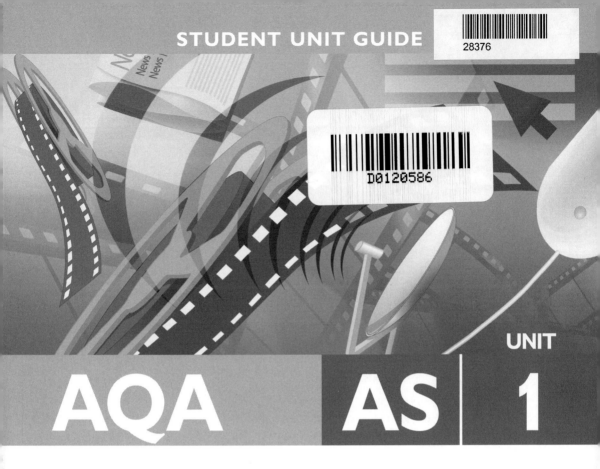

28376

D0120586

AQA | AS | UNIT 1

Media Studies

Investigating media

Martin Walker

Philip Allan Updates, an imprint of Hodder Education, an Hachette UK company, Market Place, Deddington, Oxfordshire OX15 0SE

Orders

Bookpoint Ltd, 130 Milton Park, Abingdon, Oxfordshire OX14 4SB
tel: 01235 827720
fax: 01235 400454
e-mail: uk.orders@bookpoint.co.uk

Lines are open 9.00 a.m.–5.00 p.m., Monday to Saturday, with a 24-hour message answering service. You can also order through the Philip Allan Updates website: www.philipallan.co.uk

© Philip Allan Updates 2010

ISBN 978-0-340-98715-5

First printed 2010
Impression number 5 4 3 2 1
Year 2014 2013 2012 2011 2010

This guide has been written specifically to support students preparing for the AQA AS Media Studies Unit 1 examination. The content has been neither approved nor endorsed by AQA and remains the sole responsibility of the author.

Typeset by Phoenix Photosetting, Chatham, Kent
Printed by MPG Books, Bodmin

Hachette UK's policy is to use papers that are natural, renewable and recyclable products and made from wood grown in sustainable forests. The logging and manufacturing processes are expected to conform to the environmental regulations of the country of origin.

P1732

Contents

Introduction

■ ■ ■

Content Guidance

Section A: texts, concepts and contexts (unseen text)

Section B: cross-media study

Marketing, advertising and the media

■ ■ ■

Questions and Answers

■ ■ ■

Appendices

■ ■ ■

Glossary

Introduction
About this guide

Welcome to the Philip Allan guide to AQA AS Media Studies Unit 1, Investigating Media. Unit 1 deals with the examined module of the AS. The aim of this guide is to provide an overview of the requirements for this element of the course. By reading each stage carefully, you will be able to understand exactly what the examiner is looking for when assessing Unit 1. You can then be sure that your examination answers include all that is required to get the best possible marks.

The guide is divided into the following sections:
- **Introduction** — this provides an outline of the overall assessment aims for AS Media Studies and in particular, those which relate to the AS Media Studies Unit 1. The introduction will lead you through the two components of the exam: the unseen paper and the cross-media case study. This section also describes how Unit 1 relates to the practical part of the AS, Unit 2.
- **Content Guidance** — this gives details specific to Unit 1. It outlines the requirements of each element of the assessment objectives and provides the information required in order for you to achieve the best possible results. Throughout this guide, you will find frequent references to the key media concepts.
- **Questions and Answers** — this section contains examples of A-grade and C-grade answers for both sections of the Unit 1 exam, together with advice on how to prepare for the exam and further sample questions.

How to use this guide

The key concepts
In order to meet the requirements of the exam specification, you will need to demonstrate your understanding of media platforms and the key concepts. It should be noted that any reference to media 'text' means any individual media production, such as a TV show, a newspaper, a website, a film or a radio broadcast.

The key concepts are:
- **Media forms** — the type of media text that is being studied, and how it communicates; for example how a film uses cameras, actors, situations, lighting, editing and sound to tell a story. This also covers genre and narrative.
- **Media representation** — the sorts of people and places that appear in media texts, how the texts represent certain groups of people in the real world and whether or not they are stereotyped portrayals.
- **Media institutions** — the organisations that produce, control and regulate media.
- **Media audience** — who watches, listens, reads and consumes media products, and why they do this.

People who work in the media industries do not consciously apply the key concepts every time they plan a new programme or newspaper layout. Nevertheless, they have developed a sophisticated understanding of form, style and content. Media institutions undertake regular and detailed market research because of the need to attract their target audience, and, since media productions are expensive, they take precautions to avoid expensive failures. They are conscious of the competition and of current and future trends, including the different and emerging media platforms. Without this knowledge, they would not survive in this competitive world.

The purpose of Unit 1 is for you to gain knowledge and understanding of the complex nature of media communication and production. The exam will test your ability to use the key concepts to explore and analyse different media products.

The AS specification

To achieve the AQA AS qualification in Media Studies, you must successfully meet the criteria for four assessment objectives. These are assessed through the completion of two units — Unit 1 Investigating Media and Unit 2 Creating Media. Assessment of each unit is worth 50% of the total AS.

The AQA specification sets out what teachers, learners and examiners need to know and do for the AS exam. This covers the assessment objectives, which state what students need to know and do to succeed in the AS.

The assessment objectives (AOs) for AS Media Studies are:
- **AO1** — demonstrate knowledge and understanding of the media concepts, contexts and critical debates.
- **AO2** — apply knowledge and understanding when analysing media products and processes and evaluating your own practical work, to show how meanings and responses are created.
- **AO3** — demonstrate the ability to plan and construct media products using appropriate technical and creative skills.
- **AO4** — demonstrate the ability to undertake, apply and present appropriate research.

In addition to the key concepts (media forms, media representation, media institutions and media audience) you will be expected to demonstrate knowledge and understanding of marketing and advertising, as well as values and ideology. We will explore these concepts further in the study guide.

Quality of written communication is also assessed through AO2 so you must use an appropriate written form and style for the exam, and ensure that spelling, punctuation and grammar are accurate.

Scheme of assessment

The AQA AS Media Studies course is examined in two parts:
- **Unit 1 Investigating Media** — a two-hour examination in two sections (50%).

- **Unit 2 Creating Media** — production of practical coursework projects and supporting written work (50%).

(AQA refers to the two units as MEST 1 and 2 on the exam papers.)

This guide covers Unit 1 and tells you how Unit 1 relates to Unit 2. A separate Philip Allan study guide is available for Unit 2.

Unit 1 areas of study

The AQA specification focuses on the links between different types of media. This is referred to as 'cross-media study'. It involves exploring the following three 'media platforms' and texts.

Broadcasting

This should include: TV and radio programmes, both factual and fictional; films; adverts; trailers and other audio/visual promotional material.

E-media

These should include: websites; blogs/wikis; social networks; podcasts; advertising and promotional materials; radio; television; music or film downloads; games and emerging forms (e.g. mobile phones for consuming and producing media).

Print

This should include: newspapers; magazines; advertising and marketing texts including promotional materials.

In addition, the specification states that:

> Candidates will [need to] gain a basic understanding of the role of marketing and the advertising industry in financing and promoting media through the investigation of a range of advertising texts and strategies present within and across the media platforms.

How the Unit 1 exam is structured

The table below shows how the exam is put together in two sections, how the marks are awarded and the amount of time you should spend on each answer.

Unit 1: Investigating Media, two-hour exam (marked from a total of 80 marks)

Section A: unseen text (48 marks)	Section B: cross-media study (32 marks)
View the unseen text — 15 minutes Question 1 (12 marks) — 15 minutes Question 2 (12 marks) — 15 minutes Question 3 (12 marks) — 15 minutes Question 4 (12 marks) — 15 minutest	Choose one question out of two to answer
Four questions = 1 hour and 15 minutes	One question = 45 minutes

The exam paper will advise you how much time to take on each section. As you can see, Section A has the higher marks and therefore you should spend longer answering this section, while making sure you allow the suggested time for Section B.

Section A: unseen text (48 marks)

In Section A of the exam you will be given a media text to study that you do not see until you go into the exam. The unseen text will use one of the following platforms: moving image, audio, e-media or print. The exam board gives schools, colleges and other centres some indication of which media platform the unseen text will be on. In the exam you have to answer four questions on this unseen text.

The exam paper states that you will have 15 minutes to look at the unseen text, and suggests you spend 15 minutes each on the four questions, giving a total of 1 hour and 15 minutes.

Section B: cross-media study (32 marks)

In Section B you have to prepare a case study before you go into the exam, which you should choose from a set of topics provided by AQA. In this section, you are given two questions to choose from and you must answer one of these.

It is suggested that you use the remaining 45 minutes to answer your chosen question.

The Content Guidance and Questions and Answers sections of this guide will give you plenty of ideas about the sorts of questions you may find in each part of the exam, and answers that are typical of A grade and C grade.

Guidance on Unit 1 performance

The exam board does not publish hard and fast descriptors for specific grades, but this table indicates the way that teachers and examiners make judgements about your work. It is worth noticing the key words which highlight the differences between grades.

A- and B-grade candidates characteristically:	Communicate relevant knowledge and understanding of media concepts	Sustain relevant arguments linked to media contexts and critical debates	Structure and organise their writing	Communicate content and meaning through expressive and accurate writing
E- and U-grade candidates characteristically:	Communicate some knowledge and understanding of media concepts	Make reference to media contexts and critical debates	Communicate meaning using straightforward language	

How AS Unit 1 relates to AS Unit 2

The AQA AS Media Studies specification is designed to enable you to develop analytical and critical skills about the mass media. What you learn in Unit 1 will enable you to understand the key media concepts and be able to analyse media products.

Unit 2 Creating Media is where you demonstrate, through the creation of your own practical productions, the ability to research, plan and construct media texts for two different media platforms.

From Unit 1, you will gain clear understanding of the conventions of different media texts. For example, you should be able to explain who has produced a magazine and how an article from the magazine is constructed using codes and conventions to communicate effectively to its target audience.

By knowing how real media texts are constructed, and how the key concepts apply, you should be able to create effective productions yourself. For example, analysis of a magazine article should inform you exactly how to go about producing a magazine article that could work in the real media world. AQA stresses that practical work for Unit 2 'should develop out of Unit 1 ... and enable students to pursue their own media interests within a framework of media concepts, contexts and issues ... Unit 2 should be linked to the learning in Unit 1'.

Understanding the role of advertising and marketing across the media is essential, in particular the impact this would have on your own production for Unit 2.

During the Unit 1 case study, you should explore demographics, and the way in which audiences for media products are matched to audiences for advertised products, so that advertisers can address their chosen market through scheduling and placement of adverts. This is very important for Unit 2 when you identify your target audience and explain how and where you will reach it.

Examples of Unit 1 topics and texts

The AS specification focuses on cross-media study using different media platforms.

Section A

For this section (unseen text), you will be shown or played a single media text that will be from one of the following platforms: moving image, audio, e-media or print.

Two of the unseen texts that have been used by the exam board include:
- A print advert for the Sony Playstation, advertised in the *Guardian* on a Saturday in the run up to Christmas.
- A moving-image trailer advertising Channel 4+1, shown on E4 at the time when C4+1 was being launched.

Section B

The exam board recommends that you study at least one of the following topics, and use at least three example texts for each media platform.

Broadcast or film fiction

Investigate how audio-visual broadcast or film fiction is presented across the media, primarily in broadcasting and cinema platforms, but also in newspapers and magazines, the internet and portable electronic devices.

Documentary and hybrid forms

Investigate how documentaries are presented, primarily in audio-visual broadcasting and cinema platforms, but also the treatment of these in newspapers and magazines, the internet and portable electronic devices. Explore production and reception of documentary products including the ways in which audiences may consume, participate and respond to documentaries and their coverage.

Lifestyle

Investigate how lifestyle productions in the form of make-over, information and advice products (such as buying and decorating property, cooking, slimming, bringing up children, improving a relationship, fashion tips etc.) are presented across the media, in audio-visual broadcasting, the internet, newspapers and magazines.

Music

Investigate how music is presented across the media, in audio-visual broadcasting, the internet, portable electronic devices, newspapers and specialist magazines. Study the production and reception of this coverage including the ways in which audiences may select, consume and respond to music products.

News

Investigate how news is presented across the media, in audio-visual broadcasting, newspapers including online newspapers, the internet and portable electronic devices. Study the production and reception of news, including the ways in which audiences may select, produce, respond to and contribute to news.

Sport

Investigate how sport is presented across the media, in audio-visual broadcasting, the internet, portable electronic devices, newspapers and magazines. They should study the production and reception of sport including the ways in which audiences may select, consume and respond to the coverage of sport (and sports products).

Content
Guidance

In this part of the guide we will be looking at the sort of knowledge and understanding that AQA expects you to demonstrate in the exam. We will explore this by close reference to the types of questions asked for each section.

In Section A (unseen text) you will answer one question on each of the following key concepts: media forms, media representation, media institutions and media audience. For Section B (cross-media study) you will need to prepare for questions that focus on the same concepts of media forms, representation, institutions and audience, but this time you will be relating these to your case study. When you see your exam paper, however, you will find two questions in Section B, which could be on any combination of the four key concepts, and you have to answer only one of these questions.

We'll consider the questions for each section in detail to give you plenty of ideas as to how you can approach them. Your time will be limited in the exam, so you will need to select the most important and relevant points that you want to make.

As well as explaining the structure of the exam, this section will also deal with the content. The AQA AS specification is designed so that students engage with contemporary media texts and issues. It acknowledges that the way in which we communicate through technology is constantly evolving. Innovations become part of the mainstream very quickly, and although the specification cannot predict what will emerge, it has been created with this in mind. Your ability to understand and engage with the impact of new technology on audiences and institutions is a very important aspect of the AS specification. The specification also takes into account that while audiences now create their own media content through applications like YouTube, millions still engage with older forms of media, like those who flock to see a cinematic spectacle such as *Avatar*.

Both older and emerging media forms produce a huge number of texts. This guide can only scratch the surface of what is available. However, it has been written to provide a range of clear examples that will illustrate how to explore the key concepts and issues that the exam questions will test.

Section A: texts, concepts and contexts (unseen text)

The focus of the questions

On your exam paper you will see that Section A is subtitled 'Texts, concepts and contexts'. This is because Section A is where you show your knowledge and understanding of the four key concepts by analysing a particular text that is given a very clear context, or situation, in which it exists. The text is referred to as 'unseen' because you are not allowed to know what it is and it is unlikely that you will have seen it before.

The four questions specifically ask about media forms, representation, institutions and audience in relation to the text that you are shown or played. In a moment we will look at what these concepts mean by studying the sorts of questions that you will be asked.

First of all, there are a few other additional points you need to know about Section A.

- **Avoid repetition** — when answering the four questions, you must not repeat yourself in different answers. This can be quite difficult because the four areas constantly overlap. For example, if you are talking about how the text appeals to the audience (Question 4) it would be hard to avoid discussing the language and other media forms used (Question 1), or the sort of representations that are being made (Question 2). This means that you will need to choose which question would be the most appropriate place to make your point.
- **Study a wide range of texts** — to prepare for this section you should study a wide range of different media texts from the three platforms (broadcast, e-media and print). This will give you good practice for the exam, when you will be given a text that you have not seen or heard before. The idea is that regardless of what text you are given, you should be able to analyse it effectively.
- **Use media theory relevantly** — often, in preparation for media exams, schools and colleges introduce students to key figures and major ideas in media and communication theory, such as Roland Barthes and semiotics or the Frankfurt School and the hypodermic needle model of audience reception. The AQA exam board is very clear that it does not want you to repeat names and theories for the sake of it, just to show that you know these things. What examiners are looking for is your ability to explain and discuss the key concepts in relation to the text. Any media theory that you discuss *must* have some relevance to the question and the text. For example, if you are shown a news broadcast as your unseen text, and you spend a long time explaining what you know about Propp's characters and functions theory you will not get much sympathy from the examiner. If, however, you describe how sections of the programme show images that have an authoritative voice-over explaining what the pictures mean,

and that this is an example of Barthes' ideas of anchorage, the examiner will see that you understand the concept and that you have made relevant use of a theory to develop and explain the concept further.

- **Use appropriate terminology** — finally, as we have seen before, you must remember to use appropriate media terminology in your answers

Approaching an example text

To help you understand what will happen in Section A, we'll use an unseen text example from a previous AS exam — a moving-image trailer advert for Channel 4+1. Your school or college may be able to lend you a copy of this. If not, you could try recording and watching any example of a trailer for TV services and compare it with the notes on the questions below. The questions used are examples of the types of questions you are likely to be asked, but they will probably be worded slightly differently in your exam.

To start with, you will be given a few minutes to read through the exam paper, and then given 15 minutes to study the text before you will be expected to write your answers. In the case of audio-visual texts, the text will be played three times, with 5 minutes in between for you to make notes, although you are advised not to make notes the first time it is played.

One of the most important things to notice on first reading the exam paper is that you are given a lot of very useful background contextual information about the text before you see or hear it. You will be expected to refer to and use this information in your answers. Here is what the exam paper said about the Channel 4+1 trailer advert:

> As a public service broadcaster, Channel 4 is expected to be innovative and experimental and provide a broad range of high-quality and culturally diverse programming. Programmes in this trailer include: *Ugly Betty*, *The Simpsons*, *River Cottage: Gone Fishing*, *Ramsay's Kitchen Nightmares*, *Property Ladder*, *How to Look Good Naked*, *The Secret Millionaire* and *Hollyoaks*.
>
> This trailer was broadcast on E4 during December 2007 for the launch of Channel 4+1. Channel 4+1 is available on Freeview, Sky and Virgin Media, and shows Channel 4's schedule 1 hour later than the original broadcast.

This information is extremely important, so do not ignore it. There is already a lot that can help us with answering the questions before we have even seen the text.

Question 1: media forms

Discuss the use of codes and conventions in this media text.

Question 1 is asking you to explain how the text communicates to the audience using different forms of media language. This will include the use of **genre** and

narrative as well as the different **codes** that apply and whether these codes are used conventionally or not. Let's break these things down further to clarify what you need to do.

Genres

Genres are categories of media that should be very easily recognisable to anyone, from a child to an old person, so that people can choose whether they want to engage with a particular media text or not. Part of your job in this question is to identify the genre of the text by showing what the genre signifiers are and to say whether they fulfil audience expectations or not.

In the Channel 4+1 example, we need to assess if this text is recognisable as a trailer. We can start with a quick description of the elements:

- It has a non-diegetic (not part of the action) voice-over at the start and end of the text.
- It shows a montage of clips from some well-known Channel 4 programmes.
- There is an upbeat music soundtrack that continues throughout the text.
- At certain points the diegetic (part of the action) voices of people in the texts can be heard.
- At the end there is some written text that tells us that this is from Channel 4 and where we can find this service.

These are all the signifiers of the genre, and they are conventionally used. This means it has been produced to look and sound to most people like a trailer. The audience would assume that this sort of text would provide us with information, which it does, through the voice-over and written text.

Narrative

The narrative structure also confirms the genre for us. It is a complete text, not a section, which lasts only about 1 minute. This narrows down the possibilities of what the text could be — there are relatively few moving-image texts, other than adverts, that would be so short. The narrative is time-based and linear, which means that it lasts a particular amount of time and is designed to be watched from start to finish to make full sense of it.

The trailer starts with the music soundtrack and short clips that last a few seconds each, with a voice-over asking the question 'Missed your favourite Channel 4 show?'. This is directly addressing the audience and sets up the expectation that what we are about to see and hear will present us with a resolution to the problem of missing our favourite programme. The voice-over immediately answers the question by telling us that we can now catch up by watching all our favourite programmes an hour later. This indicates that we're watching something that needs to get its message across quickly, and not build up to its resolution over an extended period of time.

The main bulk of the text is taken up by a montage of short clips that are cut together. These are mainly a mix of action shots — walking, posing, plate-smashing, kissing, laughing, fishing and eating — which are followed by reaction shots showing close-ups of people's faces appearing to react to the actions.

Narrative theory

We could support this part of the analysis with some reference to theory. One of **Barthes' ideas** about narrative codes is that, often, the audience is drawn into the story just by wanting to see what happens next in the action. In this case, the audience should fairly quickly recognise that there is no straightforward storyline, so their interest in the text is seeing recognisable characters and celebrities, such as Ugly Betty and Gordon Ramsay, acting and reacting.

We could also refer to the **Kuleshov effect**, which is where we see something in one shot and connect it to what happens in the following shot. An example of this occurs when we see a scantily clad woman from *How to Look Good Naked* followed by a close-up of the face of a male character from *Hollyoaks* giving a wide-eyed stare. Although we are aware that the clips are from entirely different programmes, we still enjoy the way that they seem to be interacting.

A final point to make is that the possible confusion of the wealth of different images presented to the audience is reduced by the continuity of the soundtrack which remains constant throughout the trailer.

Media codes

Codes refer to the parts of the text that communicate with us. A useful way of thinking about the codes is to divide them into:

- linguistic codes
- symbolic codes
- technical codes

Linguistic codes are the words that are being spoken and any writing that we see. **Symbolic codes** refer to things like body language, props, tone of voice and style of music. **Technical codes** cover aspects such as the use of close-ups, the editing or the way in which the sound is mixed. You don't need to go into lengthy explanations about what codes are, you just need to show that you recognise the different ways in which the text communicates.

Question 2: media representation

Consider the representations of people and places in this text.

This question is asking you to explore and explain how the text has been constructed using certain types of people and certain locations. The word 'constructed' is important here. We often accept what the media presents to us as if it is the only truth about the way things are. However, whether the text is about reality (e.g. news, documentary and interviews) or like reality (e.g narrative films, dramas and soap operas), someone has made decisions about what to include and what to leave out. In thinking about this question, you need to ask why the text uses the representations that it does, and what values and points of view these representations are trying to promote to the audience through the way they have been selected and constructed.

Demographic issues

Considering the representation of people and places involves thinking about demographic issues, and these are connected to the answer we will give to Question 4 about audiences. These issues include things like **gender**, **age**, **race**, **culture**, **socio-economic status**, but texts may also be dealing with wider themes such as freedom and oppression, or love and hate.

A good starting point for this sort of question is just to observe and listen. By doing this, you can state a number of things about the trailer:
- A woman is used for the voice-over.
- The clips show a mixture of documentary reality (e.g. Gordon Ramsay, Gok Wan, *Property Ladder*) and fictional reality (e.g. *Ugly Betty*, *The Simpsons*, *Hollyoaks*).
- There is a mixture of UK and US accents and programmes.
- A range of ages of people is shown, although most people are young to middle-aged adults.
- Most of the people we see appear to be white Europeans.
- Both males and females are represented.
- Some locations show people's houses, other settings include a speed boat on the sea and kitchens.

Putting representation in context

Now we need to move on to explore these representations, considering why the text has been constructed in this way. This is one of the points where the contextual information provided with the question is important. We have been told that 'Channel 4 is expected to be innovative and experimental and provide a broad range of high-quality and culturally diverse programming'. Our first point could be to examine the innovation and experimentation represented in the clip.

Gender

If we start with representations of males and females, we could look to see if the types of programmes and the way they are portrayed do more than provide us with stereotypes of gender and sexuality. On the one hand, we could say that *Ugly Betty* challenges some perceptions of having to use conventionally attractive people as stars of a show, and *How to Look Good Naked* is dealing with similar body-image issues and is presented by a gay man, which is still relatively unusual across broadcast TV. The voice-over is the authoritative voice in the trailer, and this is female.

However, when we compare the representations of gender in the trailer as a whole we can see that a lot of the images of women seem to be for male sexual pleasure, such as Marge Simpson dressed in a leotard almost lap dancing for Homer, Las

Vegas-style dancers in skimpy costumes dancing in front of Gordon Ramsay, and the images of women posing in their underwear in *How to Look Good Naked*. The idea that these are stereotyped images for the male gaze are reinforced by the editing (referred to in Question 1), where we see close-ups of male faces from different clips appearing to get pleasure from viewing the women. This view is challenged to an extent later in the trailer when we see a woman in a hard hat working on a building site.

The overall gender imbalance is reflected in the fact that the celebrity presenters shown are all male, although even in this there are apparent differences. Gordon Ramsay is the more stereotypical 'alpha male', while Hugh Fearnley-Whittingstall and Gok Wan represent other ideas of masculinity.

Cultural diversity

In the same way, we can also explore the representation of cultural diversity. If you look at Channel 4's schedules, you will see either that its programmes often represent a variety of cultures, for instance Indian films, or that it has seasons of programmes that discuss issues of race and culture directly, such as the 2009 season of documentaries *Race: Science's Last Taboo*.

The trailer hints at cultural diversity in the representations of *Ugly Betty*, where Betty represents second-generation Mexican heritage, and Gok Wan as a second-generation Asian. However, it could also be argued that the trailer prefers to represent American culture rather than significant minority cultures in the UK such as South Asian or African Caribbean.

We could conclude from viewing the representations shown that although Channel 4 does broadcast innovative, experimental and culturally diverse programming in its schedules, it has not displayed a great deal of this in the trailer. We'll consider the reasons for this when we look at institutions in Question 3 and audiences in Question 4.

Places

In considering representations of places in the trailer, we could compare glamorous settings with more ordinary locations. This opposition is already inherent in *How to Look Good Naked* where an 'ordinary' woman is transformed into a catwalk model. It can also be seen with Gordon Ramsay speeding across a sun-drenched stretch of ocean and Hugh Fearnley-Whittingstall in a rowing boat on a lake. The trailer also shows us a number of ordinary domestic settings such as the Simpsons' front room, a typical British town house being renovated in *Property Ladder* and an old couple's living room in *Secret Millionaire*.

Question 3: media institutions

What does this text tell us about the media institutions involved?

This question is asking you to show what you know about media organisations associated with the unseen text in terms of:

- their **ownership**
- their **funding**
- how they use **technology**
- how they use **marketing and advertising**

You also need to consider the **values** and **ideology** that different organisations have by exploring the ideas that guide how they operate and what sort of texts they produce.

Institutions and their contexts

As when discussing representations for Question 2, the contextual information provided on the exam paper is very useful in helping you to approach the topic of institutions. In our example, the information tells us that Channel 4 is a public service broadcaster, which means it is expected to be 'innovative and experimental and provide a broad range of high-quality and culturally diverse programming'. It also tells us that the trailer was broadcast on E4 during December 2007 for the launch of Channel 4+1, and that the service shows Channel 4's schedule 1 hour later than the original broadcast and is available on Freeview, Sky and Virgin Media.

This information gives you a lot of detail that you would not get directly from the text itself. To get a good mark for this section you need to show that you have used this information effectively. To get a very good mark, you should also add to and develop the information with your own knowledge and understanding.

Ownership and funding

In looking at ownership in this example, we are clearly dealing with Channel 4, one of the main terrestrial broadcasters in the UK. The familiar branding for Channel 4 appears at the end of the trailer to confirm this through the Channel 4 logo, which it uses to differentiate itself from the other terrestrial broadcasters.

Being a public service broadcaster (PSB) suggests that Channel 4 is publicly funded, like the BBC, through the TV licence fee to provide programming that will address and appeal to a wide range of particular audiences. However, as a media student, you will probably be aware that Channel 4 gets its funding through adverts, in the same way that ITV and Channel 5 do. This tells us that Channel 4 is a private business with the commitments of a public organisation. The written information on the exam paper points us towards this when it tells us that Channel 4 has to be innovative and experimental, and provide a broad range of high-quality and culturally diverse programming. If we consider Channel 4's schedule of programmes we can see that it has to juggle a mixture of more mainstream programmes that will appeal to a larger general audience, such as its popular game shows, with quite specific programmes that are aimed at particular demographic groups.

As a PSB, Channel 4 has had to differentiate itself from the BBC, and it has done this to a certain extent by being more innovative, cutting edge and risky in what it offers.

A lot of Channel 4 programmes can be recognised as having these qualities, and in this way we get to see some of the core values and ideologies that the broadcaster promotes.

Because Channel 4 has to be paid for by advertising, the Channel 4+1 idea seems to make good business sense, as well as providing a good service to its viewers. Presumably Channel 4 gains some financial benefit from showing the adverts that accompany the programmes on Channel 4+1, without having the cost of producing any extra programmes.

Technology and advertising

We also need to consider technological issues that institutions have to deal with. Terrestrial broadcasting means that Channel 4's services are available through signals sent out from land-based broadcast masts, rather than from satellite or cable transmission. Up until the digital switchover, it was not technically possible for the old analogue signal to broadcast more than five TV channels. The only way that viewers could have more channels was through cable or satellite, which had to be paid for, and more recently via the internet. As one of a handful of analogue terrestrial broadcasters, Channel 4 has been a relatively big player in TV broadcasting for a long time.

With the digital switchover, the company faces much greater competition with many more broadcasters, because digital signals take up far less space on the airwaves than the old analogue signals. The increasing complexity of the broadcast situation is suggested when the introduction to the trailer tells us that the service is available on Freeview, Sky and Virgin.

Clearly, Channel 4, like all the other older broadcasters, has had to offer more services to keep the audience interested as new technology has allowed more competition. In addition, they also have to address different patterns of consumption by audiences. If you went back even a decade, you would find the majority of people fitting their viewing around the schedules set by the TV companies. Changes in technology have given viewers more options to access programmes at times that suit them. The Channel 4+1 service is one example of how the company has developed an offering to make it easier for the audience to access Channel 4's services in a way that is more convenient for audience members.

It is also important to notice that this trailer is shown on E4, to advertise what is happening on Channel 4 itself. E4 is another example of how Channel 4 has had to diversify what it offers in the light of media technological developments and the resulting changes in patterns of audience consumption. E4 began as a pay TV offshoot of Channel 4 in 2001, and was offered on cable TV and Sky digital. In 2005 it became available on Freeview, and was joined at that time by More 4. E4 offers programming broadly aimed at a younger, teens-to-30 audience, while More 4 is aimed at viewers aged 30+.

The impact of institutional constraints and expectations

When we look at the Channel 4+1 trailer in the light of this information we can see how Channel 4 has produced a trailer that manages to accommodate quite effectively the many constraints and expectations with which it operates as a broadcaster.

The trailer uses clips from programmes that would bring in some bigger audiences for Channel 4, as well as appealing to the younger E4 audience. The clips are taken from programmes that are scheduled mainly in the early/mid-evening slots, when audience share is most likely to be at its greatest.

Each media platform has its own organisation for carrying out audience research on behalf of different media institutions, and it would be useful for you to mention this, even if you cannot give actual figures for the unseen text (the different audience research organisations are listed in Appendix 2). In this example, we could say that many of the programmes being used in the trailer would probably have appeared in the Broadcast Audience Research Board's (BARB) top 30 most-watched Channel 4 programmes at some point.

The use of certain celebrity presenters, for instance Gordon Ramsay and Gok Wan, along with shows like *The Simpsons*, *Hollyoaks* and a programme such as *Ugly Betty* which has **high production values**, will have popular appeal, in particular to the E4 audience.

It could be argued that as well as advertising the Channel 4+1 service, the trailer is also using clips from these popular programmes to promote Channel 4 content more generally. This can be seen as an example of **synergy**, where one media product (or in this case a number of Channel 4's main texts) is used to promote another product (Channel 4+1). Synergy can also work across platforms, for example where a film uses a track from a well-known group. In this case, the film promotes the group, and the group helps to promote the film each time the track is played.

Even though the trailer has gone for some big names and audience-grabbing clips, it also manages to promote some of its **public service values** as well. *Ugly Betty* and *How to Look Good Naked* challenge stereotypes of conventional beauty and sexuality, while *Secret Millionaire* and *Property Ladder* have some innovative perspectives on socio-economic status.

However, as we saw in our exploration of representation, there is a sense that the trailer is playing it safe in how far it shows the **cultural diversity** of which Channel 4 is capable as a broadcaster. Knowing what we do about Channel 4 as an institution, we can see why this is. It has to juggle being a PSB with being a commercially successful business. So it makes sense that the trailer uses some of the channel's more popular programmes to advertise its services, and these at least show some degree of cultural diversity and therefore reflect Channel 4's values as a broadcaster.

Question 4: media audience

Explore some of the ways this text communicates with its target audience.

Your response to this question will require you to:

- identify the likely target audience
- analyse the text to explain how it appeals to the target audience
- explore how new technology allows audiences to respond in different ways to the media

Describing an audience in demographic terms

To describe an audience successfully you need to be familiar with **demographic terms**. These are ways of dividing the audience up into different groupings of people. The most commonly used terms are **age** and **gender**. At AS, you should be able to extend this through understanding that media producers and advertisers (who use the media to reach potential customers for their products and services) think in much more detail about how their target audience is made up. A fuller list of demographic descriptions is in the Glossary. As we go through this section you will start to pick up a variety of different terms.

How to identify the audience

Using the text and background material

By looking at and listening to the text, and reading the background information given in the introduction to this section on the exam paper, you should be able to come to a fairly accurate estimation of who the producers intended the audience to be. In the Channel 4+1 trailer, we are told in the exam introduction that it was broadcast on E4. If you don't know anything about E4 then this will not be of much help, but the examiners will assume that, as you are studying media, you have some idea about the audience at which E4 is aimed. As we saw in the institutions section, this is teens and young adults.

Even without knowing much about E4, you can still look at the introductory information and learn something about the audience. The fact that Channel 4 creates 'innovative and experimental...and culturally diverse programming' tells us quite a lot about the sorts of people to whom the channel is appealing. So, just by looking at the exam paper we have worked out that the intended audience is teens and young adults who will probably want something different from run-of-the-mill, mainstream programming, which could in turn suggest that they may have a higher level of education. In addition, they may come from or be interested in a variety of different cultures.

Using the representations

We can then move on to look at the representations for further clues about the target audience. Often, in media texts, the majority of representations will reflect elements of the audience being targeted, for instance age and gender. *Hollyoaks* represents mainly teens and young adults, but some of the characters are members of families with older and younger people. This is also seen in *The Simpsons*. *Ugly Betty* and *How to Look Good Naked* have ordinary women at the centre. *River Cottage* and *Ramsay's Kitchen Nightmares* show men who feel comfortable being in the kitchen. *Property Ladder* and *Secret Millionaire* deal with socio-economic status, which is a way of describing what sort of income people have and what impact that has on their social lives. *Property Ladder* deals with homeowners, while *Secret Millionaire* contrasts wealthy people who have a comfortable lifestyle with poorer people at the other end of the socio-economic scale.

Bringing the factors together

In most media texts, age and gender may be the primary demographic considerations for producers in appealing to the audience. However, we can see from the trailer for Channel 4+1, from the expectations of Channel 4 as a broadcaster, and from the representations being made that there is greater subtlety and complexity in the way that this audience is being attracted. So, as well as being male and female, and aged between 16 and 30 years, the E4 target audience is likely to be:

- educated to further- or higher-education level
- from a skilled or professional family background
- to have some disposable income and leisure time
- to have values and interests beyond the mainstream culture

How the text appeals to the audience

Having identified how we think the target audience is made up, we can move on to consider what it is within the unseen text that will appeal to people. One of the interesting things about the Channel 4+1 trailer is that it does not specifically demonstrate the benefit of the service that Channel 4 is offering. If this were the case, then the advert would probably show someone missing their favourite programme, being initially frustrated, then being overjoyed to discover that they can watch after all an hour later. Instead, the trailer reminds the audience about some of Channel 4's most popular shows, with information about how the Channel 4+1 service works topping and tailing the trailer. Part of the appeal for the audience is that Channel 4 is considering their needs by giving them even more convenient access to what they want.

Media theory: uses and gratification model

This is another point where you could usefully apply some relevant media theory. The **uses and gratification model** of how audiences use and consume media argues that audiences actively seek out media texts for their own personal satisfaction. As more mass media became available to audiences towards the end of the twentieth century, viewers, readers and listeners had more choice. By considering audiences from the perspective of this model, we can look at the pleasure or satisfaction people get from a media text.

One area that illustrates this is the tension between people wanting to see aspects of their ordinary lives in the media, while at the same time wanting to see things that they can dream of or aspire to and that seem impossible to achieve. As we have already discussed in our exploration of representation, the Channel 4+1 trailer plays on this tension well, by showing plenty of ordinary people in ordinary situations, from *The Simpsons* to people engaged in DIY building projects, contrasted with the high-class fashion world of *Ugly Betty*, and a rich, famous celebrity chef zooming across the ocean in a speed boat.

Narrative construction

The audience also gets pleasure out of the narrative construction of media texts. This may be through the tingle of anticipation in wanting to see how a cliff-hanger ending will be resolved, to predicting and anticipating how certain relationships between people will develop. In the trailer, the audience will get pleasure from seeing well-known characters and situations from completely different programmes interacting with each other. We looked at the Kuleshov effect earlier, and the audience for this trailer would enjoy some of the narrative jokes that come about through juxtaposing (putting two unrelated things together) different characters through montage editing.

How audiences use technology

Finally, we need to think about how new technology is adopted and used by audiences. Media are all about communication through technology. Broadly speaking, there have been three waves of media technology. This started in the late Middle Ages with print. It took a relatively long time for people to engage fully with this new method of communication using multiple reproductions of the same message. The second wave came with a raft of inventions in the nineteenth and twentieth centuries. Some were reproductive technologies, such as photography, cinema and sound recording. At this time came the new broadcast technologies of radio and television, which could reach huge audiences simultaneously. The third wave has been the digital revolution, which has introduced new ways of communicating, like the internet, while also transforming all the previous technologies.

As audiences have taken on new media technologies, they have become more sophisticated in their demands about what media can and should provide. The accelerating speed of change is a key feature. Print took centuries to become firmly established, whereas these days we laugh at how cumbersome and limited a mobile phone seems from five years ago compared with the latest model.

Innovation adoption cycle

In the 1960s a man called Everett Rogers came up with a model to describe how human beings take on new ideas and technologies. He called it the **innovation adoption curve**. He showed that a few people are **innovators** — the people who will risk taking on new ideas and technology that is not fully proven. They are followed by a slightly bigger group called the **early adopters**, who have seen what the innovators are up to, and are willing to take a risk. Then comes the **early majority**, which makes up about a third of a population. By now there is a kind of snowball effect, and the technology or idea is considered to be successful, so the **late majority** feels safe to join in, and what was new becomes acceptable to around 80% of the population. Finally come the **laggards**, who for various reasons need much longer to be convinced that their lives would be improved by some new-fangled device or idea.

What seems to be happening currently with media technology is that the innovation adoption cycle is happening more quickly. Media producers constantly have to update and offer new services as consumers adopt the latest technology. Channel 4+1 now seems to be a well-established idea that has subsequently been extended across other Channel 4 offerings, such as E4+1. What is important to notice in this unseen example text is that when Channel 4 was launching its new service, it saw the younger audience of E4 as having more potential to take the risk of using this new way of receiving broadcasts.

This may well be because innovators and early adopters tend to be younger people with disposable income (i.e. money to spend beyond basic living costs) who like ideas and products that are 'innovative and experimental' (which is how the exam paper described Channel 4 as a broadcaster). You can see this same pattern with all sorts of media technology from mobile phones to computer games and new ways of viewing films or listening to music. The equipment tends to be expensive initially, but its capabilities appeal to the spontaneity, appetites and needs of younger people.

The unseen text and new technology issues
It is most likely that the unseen text you will be given in Section A of the exam will be up to date, and will therefore be affected in some way by issues of new technology. The issues will either concern media technology that is adapting to incorporate new innovations, such as broadcast TV switching to digital, or older technologies that are threatened by change, such as newspapers that are losing readership, having to go online and being forced to give away their content because audiences don't expect to have to pay for media on the internet.

Section B: cross-media study

In this section you will use the information and analysis from your cross-media case study to answer one of two questions. Your case study will explore the presence of media texts, the way they are produced and how they are received across three different platforms. For example, you may start by studying fictional texts for broadcast TV, then go on to explore how these TV texts are treated on the internet and in newspapers. You should have at least three different textual examples that can be tracked across the three platforms. Below we'll look at some examples that could be used for each of the six topics.

The focus of the questions

In Section B you have to answer one question from a choice of two. Whichever question you choose, you will be expected to provide a longer, more detailed answer than for the questions in Section A. The two questions will be general rather than specifically about the case study topic areas — for example 'Account for the similarities and differences in the codes and conventions used in the media products from your case study'. As you can see, this means that each question will be relevant whether you have studied, say, broadcast or film fiction or the presentation of music in the media.

One of the key points to remember is that this section is asking you to consider how the production and reception of media texts increasingly use different platforms, and to demonstrate how the cross-platform connections are being made.

You will be expected to show your knowledge and understanding of media concepts and the contexts, or situations, in which they are both created by producers and received by the audience. The two questions for Section B will focus on the same key concepts as Section A:

- **Media forms** — the question may ask you to explain codes and conventions, narrative and generic features of each cross-media text.
- **Institutions** — you could be asked to give the reasons why producers make the texts available across the different platforms, and consider the use of marketing.
- **Representation** — you may need to consider who is being represented and how the representations are influenced and changed by the different platforms being studied.
- **Audience** — which may include how people consume media texts as well as their ability to interact with, and even extend production of, the texts using different platforms.

You need to prepare for all four areas. This is because you must show that you can 'think on your feet' — you won't know exactly what the questions will ask, and you need to be able to adapt what you know about your case study from the point of view of each of the four key concepts. It is not a good strategy just to prepare for one or two key concepts because the questions may not ask about them. You can only be fully prepared if you can apply all the key concepts to your case study.

Advice on answering questions

When answering the question you should start with a very brief outline of your case study so the examiner understands exactly what you are referring to in your answer. You must then relate the question to the media products that you have studied, and make sure that you support your answer with plenty of reference to examples from your case study that are relevant to the question. You should aim to write around 600 words in your answer.

It is also worthwhile remembering that the assessment is based on the following assessment objectives:

- **AO1** — demonstrate knowledge and understanding of media concepts, contexts (and critical debates).
- **AO2** — apply knowledge and understanding when analysing media products and processes to show how meanings and responses are created.

Approaching the case study

Earlier we looked at the topic areas that could be studied for Unit 1. To remind you, the topic areas are: broadcast or film fiction, documentary and hybrid forms, lifestyle, music, news and sport. In this section we will be exploring how to create a case study based on those topics and how they need to be made relevant for the sort of questions that you will be asked.

Here is a list of what your case study should include:
- It should be focused on one of the topic areas.
- It must look at media products across **at least three media platforms.**
- It must use at least **three different example texts** across the platforms.
- It needs to consider the key concepts: **media forms, representation, institutions** (including marketing) and **audience**.

Now we will look at the topics and see how you can create a case study containing three example texts that will cover the key concepts and the three media platforms.

Using the case study material in this guide

If you are following an AS Media Studies course at a school or college then you will probably be studying case studies set by your tutors. Different schools and colleges will take different approaches, for example you may study two of the topics, which will give you some choice about which case study you use in the exam. Whatever your situation, this guide will give you clear directions about what to expect so that you can be fully prepared, and this should complement what you are studying in school or college.

We will look at all six suggested case study topics, but we will particularly explore the first two — broadcast or film fiction, and documentary and hybrid forms — in detail. This is mainly because the case studies contain many common elements that would be repeated, but also because these topics tend to be popular with students and schools or colleges. So, even if you are not intending to use broadcast or film fiction, or documentary and hybrid forms, it is recommended that you read these sections. The broadcast or film fiction section will use some textual examples. It will focus more, however, on how you can think about the different media platforms with particular reference to the way in which institutions and audiences have adapted to digital media, especially the internet, as a revolutionary new media platform. The documentary and hybrid forms section will focus more on specific textual examples to support understanding of how the case study can explore different platforms while focusing on the key concepts.

Topic 1: broadcast or film fiction

For this topic you need to take three textual examples that are either film or broadcast fictional texts. There is an enormous range of texts available for study, representing different genres and subject matter. Let's take the following examples from each platform:

Film fiction

Quantum of Solace (Eon Productions)
Slumdog Millionaire (Pathé/Celador/Film 4)
Angus Thongs and Perfect Snogging (Nickelodeon Pictures)

Broadcast fiction

FlashForward (Channel 5 TV)
Hollyoaks (Channel 4 TV)
The Archers (BBC Radio 4)

Relating key concepts to the texts

Forms

Initially, you need to be able to explore the key concepts in relation to these texts, showing your understanding of how the texts communicate using the media forms of:

- Moving image — covering aspects such as genre, narrative structure, *mise-en-scène,* performance, lighting, cinematography, editing and sound.
- Radio — also covering genre and narrative, but with more focus on speech, tone, sound effects, proximity, recording and mixing techniques, soundtrack and silence.

Through your study of this topic, you should learn a great deal about generic conventions, including typical character types, *mise-en-scène*, narrative, iconography and themes. Your study of narrative should also introduce you to Todorov, Propp and Barthes, narrative identification and the role of the narrator, and narrative techniques such as ellipsis, stretch, summary and real time.

Representation

You should show what you know about representation in each text — for example the way in which the male machismo of the Bond character has changed so much that in *Quantum of Solace* Bond does not have a sexual relationship with the lead female. You could explore the tension between family relationships and work demands in *FlashForward*, and the impact of rural issues on the central characters in *The Archers.*

Institutions

Your case study should also cover the institutions associated with each text, such as Eon productions and the James Bond franchise, ABC Studios and the way that Channel 5 scheduling is dominated by US TV dramas, or exploring how *The Archers* has been a flagship show on BBC Radio 4 for around 60 years, and still commands a healthy 4.5 million listeners each week.

Audience

Finally, you would explore the demographic features of the audience for each text and how and why they consume each text. Audience study may refer to the range of theories, such as the **uses and gratification model** through which you explore how the character of Bond provides different pleasures for male and female viewers. The **two-step flow model**, which looks at how opinion leaders influence the media, might be used to explore how word-of-mouth and press critics' endorsement spreads the popularity of a TV series as much as the marketing carried out by the TV station. Or you could consider if the **hypodermic needle model**, which suggests the media have a very powerful influence over the audience, is relevant to the way that _The Archers_ promotes certain middle-class values.

Exploring texts across platforms

Having created a good foundation based in the initial topic area, you need to explore how these sorts of texts extend beyond the areas of cinema and broadcast TV or radio, and utilise other media platforms. You should focus on following the initial broadcast or film fiction examples you started with, but there is no reason why you shouldn't use other examples to show how film and broadcast fiction extends beyond its initial platform. As you look at other media platforms, you need to remember that the focus is still on the key concepts.

All the topics suggested by AQA for the case study relate to the traditional media platforms which all have well-established formats and texts. For example, cinema has been creating fictional narratives for over a century and news has been part of the media since the earliest equivalents of newspapers were printed from carved stone blocks in eighth-century China. It is likely that your case study will start from one of these older, more established platforms.

It makes very good sense, however, to explore e-media, especially internet and website platforms. As we will discover, the relatively recent impact of this technology has been profound on producers and audiences alike. The older media platforms like TV and print have not gone away, but they have been transformed by the digital revolution. So, exploring how the producers and audiences for your example texts have been influenced by this new media technology fits perfectly with AQA's intention that students should study texts across different media platforms.

Differences between older technologies and new media platforms

Before we look at e-media in relation to our example texts, we need make sure we understand some of the technical differences between the older technologies and the newer media platforms, and see what sort of impact this has had on media producers and media audiences. In this next section, we'll particularly discuss the relationship between broadcasters, their audiences and digital technology. However, this should hopefully illustrate to you that all other media platforms have had to embrace this new technology in their own ways.

There are some fundamental differences between the technology of moving image and audio compared to websites:

- Film and broadcast forms are time-based and linear, which means that to fully understand them you should watch and/or listen from the beginning to the end. Websites are non-linear, which means that you can read, watch and listen in any order you choose, and there is no set amount of time for which you are supposed to stay on the site.
- A website can also be described as a convergent technology; this means it brings together existing technologies into one place. Websites can be read like print texts, but also show and play moving image and audio. In addition, they allow direct communication between users, e.g. telephone conversations and conference calls.

Implications of new media for producers and audiences

These multiple technical capabilities have different implications for media producers and media audiences.

Media producers for all media platforms are aware of the **increased fragmentation of the audience**. This means that the audience is no longer accessing and consuming media in predictable mass blocks. Huge amounts of choice in all areas of the media mean audiences are no longer constrained by what is on offer, or by brand loyalty. This is particularly pertinent for broadcasting, which has had to utilise the e-media platform in order to keep audiences consuming its products. To understand why this is the case, we need to look briefly at the history of broadcasting and what it has offered to audiences over the last century.

History of broadcasting

In the early twentieth century the BBC had a monopoly on the new technologies of radio and TV broadcasting in the UK. The audience could only watch and listen to what the BBC produced at the time it decided to schedule its programmes. This slowly changed with the advent of commercial broadcasting — first in TV in the 1950s, then in radio in the 1970s. Commercial broadcasting gave the audience alternative content to that offered by the BBC, but viewers and listeners were still controlled by the schedulers. Later, airwave bandwidth — that allows radio and TV signals to be sent — became fully used up, which put a limit on the number of broadcasting channels available. However, recording technology on audio cassette and later video tape allowed audiences to record programmes, giving people some choice about when they would listen and watch.

In the late 1970s and 1980s, the availability of films on video meant that for the first time people could watch fairly current feature-length movies at home without having to wait for TV companies to broadcast them. This availability coincided with the low point of cinema attendance in the UK. Some commentators predicted that cinema-going would become obsolete.

The cinema industry started to claw back its audience through the construction of multiplex cinemas built like out-of-town shopping centres in locations with easy access and parking. A trip to the cinema was rebranded as part of an entertaining family-and-friends trip to a place that had other leisure facilities. Cinema audiences have increased ever since.

Meanwhile, terrestrial broadcasters, who had been protected by the limits of broadcast bandwidth, came under fire from cable and satellite broadcasting, which not only gave audiences far more choice of content, but also got away with charging people for the privilege, while still gaining advertising revenue. However, audiences were still constrained by broadcasting schedules.

As the digital technology revolution began to occur in the 1990s, all broadcasters (whether terrestrial, satellite or cable) could see that this would lead to audiences having an even greater choice of channels and stations, and that people could start to demand services that would fit their personal lifestyles rather than follow institutional scheduling. Since the 1990s, broadcasters have had to embrace digital technology, often without fully knowing what it would lead to. The BBC, Channel 4 and Sky, in particular, have taken these challenges head on. The BBC was very quick off the mark, developing a web presence that went through a number of rebrands until it arrived at **www.bbc.co.uk**

Convergence between broadcasting, telecommunications and digital computing

There are two key technological developments that have brought about this convergence — broadband and digital television. The internet had similar problems to terrestrial TV, in that the available space — the bandwidth — to send information to users was not big enough. This meant that even sending something like a photograph would take a long time, so sending moving images and sound was very difficult. Broadband technology changed this, so that far bigger files could be sent quickly. Channel 4 was quick to use this opportunity to create whole new internet-based channels such as E4, which it could not broadcast by traditional means. When traditional analogue services switched to digital, Channel 4 was able to revert to offering these new channels as part of its TV-based broadcasts.

As a satellite broadcaster, Sky is used to providing its customers with a reception box that unscrambles the services they pay for. With developments in digital recording techniques, Sky has been able to offer an extra service within the Sky+ box — an example of a personal video recorder (PVR). This is another instance of finding ways to keep audiences who no longer stick to the broadcast schedules. PVRs have taken the idea of video recording a lot further. One of the advantages of this is that viewers can start watching a recording before the entire programme has finished. Sky has promoted this as the ability to 'pause live TV', which is somewhat inaccurate, because the England football team, or the *X Factor* contestants are not literally going to stand around waiting for you to make a cup of tea, but it has worked as a piece of marketing. The use of hard-drive technology in Sky+'s recorder has also allowed users to store large amounts of programming to watch at their own convenience without the need for messy tapes or discs.

The BBC has had almost a century of developing services and dealing with competitors trying to take over the broadcasting world that it once dominated. This experience would probably explain why the corporation has invested such a huge amount of its licence fee in developing its digital services since the 1990s, most particularly in the BBC iPlayer. This software has been one of the most successful examples of convergence so far. It has allowed the BBC to continue producing the sort of broadcast output that its audience expects while also freeing people up from its scheduling, by giving them 'on demand' programming without the need for recording. Other companies, such as BT and Virgin, have led the innovators and early adopters in merging the screen-based technologies of computers and TVs, but it is the iPlayer that has encouraged the early and late majorities to embrace fully the convergence the two.

New media technology: the shift from audiences to users

The adoption of media innovations

As with most new technology, it tends to take a while for media innovations to settle down and for people to appreciate fully what is possible. In some cases, the people who create the technology, and their financial backers, can actually hold up further development.

Inventors and entrepreneurs get the ball rolling, but they are often not the best people to develop the technology's potential. Take Thomas Edison, a prolific inventor, who was at the forefront of developing cinema at the end of the nineteenth century in the USA. Instead of sharing this new technology, he wanted to control it by taking out restrictive patents and making people pay to use his equipment and systems. This was an early example of **vertical integration**, where one company controls all stages of the process of production and distribution of media, and squeezes out any competition. Edison did this until the government stopped him, freeing up American cinema for the different ideas and creativity of others.

Another aspect of introducing new media technology is that people don't quite know what to do with it, and tend to get it to do what the previous technology has done. We can see this with the development of the internet in the 1990s. To start with, the equipment was a convergence of the familiar — a combination of a typewriter, a TV and a telephone attached to a computer. There was some sense of interactivity, with facilities like e-mail, but on the whole people used the internet as a more convenient way, with greater choice, of accessing media that was still being produced by professionals for the masses, following old models of media communication where the audience is seen as a relatively passive receiver of media messages. In addition, creating a website tended to require expertise and expensive programmes and hosting.

There was a lot of hype about how this new communication technology would grow. It was like a gold rush, with investors looking for the next big thing. Legendary stories abounded, for instance that Friends Reunited was started in someone's spare bedroom and grew to be worth millions. This was known as the '.com bubble', where huge amounts of money were invested in any new website idea going, in the hope that they would take off. The bubble burst in 2001 when investors realised that too many of the ideas were going nowhere. This was a classic part of the cycle of technological innovation.

User-generated content and Web 2.0

The internet, as we know, continued to be a powerful new medium. New ideas and technological developments expanded this platform in more effective ways. The internet started to become a technology for participation, interactivity and audience creativity, allowing people to make their own content rather than relying purely on professionals. This is called **user-generated content**, or UGC. Notice the way that the word 'audience' is shifting to the term 'users'. With new media technology, the distinctions between media producers and media audiences are increasingly blurred. This is important, because one of the things you must show in your AS exam is an understanding of how audiences engage with media, and how the digital revolution has started to change this fundamentally.

This second internet wave is often referred to as **Web 2.0**. It describes new software possibilities, as well as new ways of communicating, that are cheaper, more participative, more democratic and give a greater sense of being part of a community. The software applications work on the internet, rather than just on a computer. This means users can make use of the applications without having to buy the software to create them. (In addition there is now a lot of what is called 'open-source' software, where the code is freely available for anyone to use and distribute.) These applications are designed to be simple to use. From them we get things like social networking, video-sharing sites, wikis and blogs (see below). Most users are more familiar with successful brand names associated with the applications: MySpace, YouTube, Wikipedia, and Twitter.

Web 2.0 allows users to create and then post their own productions — it could be as simple as a blog or written response, or more complex, like uploading their own videos. YouTube is currently considered to be the world's largest UGC video-on-demand system. The quality of the images is reminiscent of early cinema when it emerged in Edison's time. It is interesting to see that it is not quality that audiences are interested in — if they want that they can go to the cinema. Members of the global audience are interested in the entirely different concept of producing and distributing their own work and ideas, and consuming each other's texts. Quality takes second place, because that can develop later.

UGC sites are developing new ways of creating, consuming and interacting with media. They empower users to be more creative, as well as generating new business and institutional opportunities.

If we now come back to our original purpose of seeing the internet as an extension of a film set, we can see how the ideas associated with Web 2.0 can apply to the specific film audience.

Websites as extensions of the source material

Official sites for film or broadcast fiction texts provide extension to the source material:

- They can be used as **advanced marketing** devices by creating anticipation among audiences of what is to come.
- They can also provide **longevity** to the original text, keeping it alive long after its original release or broadcast, which allows the audience the opportunity to reflect and evaluate what has been seen or heard.

By looking at these official sites, we can see how websites continue the media forms of the original text, such as narrative and generic conventions.

These sites can't really change the plots of the source fictions, but they are places where aspects of the storyline and characters can be discussed, further explained or added to. However, while the fictional reality of the source text can be extended to the official website, the carefully constructed original world can also be undermined by features such as interviews with the actors who play the characters, or the producers, or explanations of the production techniques being used. These things give away the constructed nature of the original text, but this sort of knowledge and information is often what audiences want. It can also prove problematic. In the case of radio, in particular, the revelation of the image of the actors who play certain roles can be disturbing for members of the audience. This is because they have created their own image of what each fictional character looks like, and they may find that the real person playing the role looks totally different.

The official sites for *Quantum of Solace* and *The Archers* offer various extensions. The Bond site, **www.007.com**, gives visitors the chance to play the character of Bond in a number of games based around themes and characters from the film. One of the features of *The Archers'* dedicated pages on **www.bbc.co.uk** offers the opportunity to work your way around an interactive map, allowing listeners to see exactly how the locations that exist in their minds relate to each other.

Audience involvement and its implications

As we have seen, one of the most important things about the internet is the possibility for the audience to create and spread its own ideas and products in relation to the original film or broadcast fictional texts. The most obvious example is the opportunity to contribute to blogs and participate in online forums.

Academics who observed media audiences in the twentieth century noted that most people consuming media did not have a sense of themselves as a whole group because although they were using the media *en masse*, they would be involved anonymously and in isolation. For example, BARB figures tell us that around 8–10 million people watch soap operas like *EastEnders* and *Coronation Street* on a daily basis, but the people who make up the audience do not have direct communication with each other, or with the producers of the programmes.

This follows the old model of communication, where media producers create messages through media texts that are distributed to audiences, who receive the messages through the different media platforms. The old model favours the producers, because there is no feedback or extension of the communication for the audience.

By participating in blogs and online forums, members of the audience are choosing to be active participators in the communication. People no longer have to be passive and isolated, because there is the possibility of dialogue. Viewers, readers and listeners can get a real sense of being part of an audience through sharing ideas, discussions and criticisms interactively.

Official internet sites tend to appeal to what we might call the **casual audience**, who may have some further interest in extending the original fictional text, and sharing their opinion. Beyond this, we can find unofficial internet sites that are not institutionally controlled or affiliated with the producers of the original text. These sites tend to appeal to audience members who have much more than just a passing interest. We could call such people **fans**, hardcore or **cult fans** and **aficionados** (devoted fans of particular media texts, genres and associated people — they tend to know every fact and snippet of information about their subject).

Unofficial websites for media texts allow such fans to communicate with each other without any filtering or censorship from the institutions that originally produced the texts. By contributing to these sites, people know that they are addressing and are in dialogue with others who share their passion and depth of interest in the text.

Before the internet, groups of fans, such as Trekkies (*Star Trek* fans) or *Star Wars* fans, would have to communicate through **fanzines** (print products produced by and for fans) or by going to conventions.

Blogs (where people continually update online news or diaries), **forums** (where users contribute to online discussions with other users) and **wikis** (websites that allow easy addition of new pages, usually for shared information) are all simple examples of UGC. Through these, the audience participates in creating new material that extends the original text for other people to view and respond to. By doing this they no longer feel isolated, but in direct communication with others who share their interest. The film review website Rotten Tomatoes, for example, gives users the opportunity to write reviews, give their personal ratings of films, write blogs, create lists of favourite films, and create and join in discussion groups.

Some websites extend the active participation and creative possibilities of UGC beyond just words. The *Angus Thongs and Perfect Snogging* site, for example, allows fans of the film to upload photos from their phones.

User-generated content and marketing campaigns
Some media producers and their marketing associates will adopt UGC from fans into their marketing campaigns. They see the power of audience participation through the internet and are creating ways to tap into it. At a simple level, viral marketing uses what is called '**social networking potential**' to encourage people to share information about a brand or product via e-mail and social networking sites. Moving on from this is the use of **widgets**. Here, a piece of information or an advert is made into an easily copied item (the widget) that the audience can paste into their own pages of a site like MySpace. A more sophisticated example concerns the film *Cloverfield*. When this was released on DVD the producers, Paramount, launched a

user-generated video contest to get fans to create a *Cloverfield*-style fictional video account of what they were doing when the monster attacked.

The print platform

The other platform that we could consider for our case study on broadcast or film fiction is print. Because this is the oldest media technology we find ourselves back to the older model of very limited interactive communication, although, as we shall see, this does not mean to say that audience consumption of these texts is purely passive.

Before the arrival of the internet, print was an obvious place where film companies and broadcasters would extend and promote their texts. This can still be seen with the BBC which produces a number of official magazine publications through its subsidiary BBC Magazines. These either deal with actual texts, such as *Dr Who* and *Top Gear*, or with genres of programme such as *BBC Music Magazine* or *BBC Gardening Magazine*.

Specialist magazines

More common than official print products are specialist magazines for specific media platforms and genres. Film magazines, such as *Empire*, *Total Film* or the independent publication *Little White Lies* (funded by the UK Film Council) provide information, news and evaluation of film for more interested members of the audience, from fans to aficionados. A magazine like *Sight and Sound* appeals to a more academic audience, who would be interested in film theory, and wider historical and cultural contexts that impact on film texts.

More easily available for broadcast fiction are soap opera magazines, such as *Inside Soap*, which aim to give soap opera fans advance information on plots and more background information on characters and the actors who play them. The appeal of soap opera magazines is rather more like tabloid newspapers, although more focused on the soap opera genre, and we'll look at tabloids below.

These specialist magazines provide a useful bridge between producers and audiences. Film and broadcast producers will usually be willing to provide content, in the form of photo stills from unreleased movies or shows, interviews with stars and so on. They do this because they know it is a useful marketing activity. However, what they cannot control is the way the magazine reviews and criticises their products.

Although these publications don't give the audience much opportunity to interact beyond a letters page, they do give people the gratification of being part of an elite group. This is because they are given exclusive access to detailed information about new releases, stars and producers. Unlike the internet, where access to official sites is easy and free, the audience members who purchase specialist magazines can feel they have invested in the right to specialist information and opinion that is not available to everyone.

Newspapers

On the other hand, newspapers provide more generalised information and opinion to a wider audience. Newspaper coverage of film and broadcast fiction tends to be divided into two categories:

- items deemed to be newsworthy
- items treated as cultural information

Heath Ledger's death just after the filming of *Batman: The Dark Knight* was an example of the production of the text becoming newsworthy, whereas a review of the film by a newspaper's film critic would be seen as part of the paper's popular cultural content.

Tabloid newspapers will often treat the star persona or celebrity as being newsworthy. While Heath Ledger's death would have gone into all types of newspapers, only the tabloids would report on something like Daniel Craig's drunken behaviour at a party as hard news.

The representation of star personas in the tabloids, and their relationship to audience and producers, is interesting and complex. Audiences relate to stars in a variety of ways; they have roles as fictional characters in films, and on TV and radio shows, yet we also see them being shown as real people in the press. This apparent 'real' side of a star is, however, just a further media representation. Very few of us get to meet and build any kind of actual relationship with someone who is a star. What we read in a newspaper is just a journalist's interpretation of who this person is, which will be heavily influenced by the star's own PR (public relations) management.

In socio-economic terms, film stars (especially those involved in Hollywood), and to a lesser extent TV and radio stars, are afforded the status once given to the upper classes. On the one hand, tabloid newspapers elevate stars as famous and wealthy demi-gods of whom audiences are in awe and who people aspire to resemble. On the other hand, tabloid journalists and editors thrive on spreading salacious gossip and exposés of immoral or illegal behaviour in an attempt to bring stars crashing down to earth.

For many media producers, the relationship with tabloid newspapers is a form of **symbiotic co-dependency**. This means that film and broadcast media institutions have to tolerate the tabloids using their productions for content for newspapers. It also means that these same institutions need and use the tabloids to market and promote their products. Media producers also know that audiences either expect stars to behave badly at some point, or that they will forgive moral lapses if the star is still able to perform well. It seems that it is only certain transgressions, such as murder or paedophilia, that the tabloids and their audiences will absolutely not allow stars to get away with. This was the case when the tabloids played a significant role in the ending of Chris Langham's career, the actor who had been a central character in BBC 2's comedy fiction *The Thick of It* when he was prosecuted for paedophile activity, even though he later won an appeal against his conviction.

Topic 2: documentary and hybrid forms

Our example texts for this topic are:

Anvil! The Story of Anvil (feature-length cinema documentary; The Works)

His Infernal Majesty (radio documentary; BBC Radio 1)

The Apprentice ('reality TV'; BBC TV)

As you can see from the choice of example texts, this topic is similar to topic 1 because it tends to use film and broadcast forms, although it would be possible to include examples of documentary writing and photo journalism in print forms.

It is useful straight away to make the distinction between the representations of reality found in factual texts as opposed to those found in fictional texts.

- Some media forms are concerned with creating texts that are *about* reality (e.g. news, current affairs, documentaries, interviews, features etc.).
- Others are interested in making texts *like* reality (e.g. films, soap operas, dramas etc.).

Your work on this case study should look at both of the following areas:

- The historical development of the documentary form.
- Some of the different modes of documentary making such as expository, observational, reflexive, or drama documentary.

The development of documentary form

To an extent you will be able to understand the different forms of documentary by exploring some of the key developments and figures associated with it such as Robert Flaherty, Dziga Vertov, John Grierson, Leni Riefenstahl and Humphrey Jennings in the early twentieth century; innovators in the mid- to late-twentieth century like the Maysles brothers and Nick Broomfield; and the documentary film maker as performative personality such as David Attenborough, Michael Moore and Louis Theroux.

By studying these figures you will also find out about documentary film-making movements such as the documentarists in the 1930s and *cinéma vérité* from the 1960s.

Codes and conventions

By studying the historical context of documentary it is possible to pick out some of the codes and conventions of the form. Here are examples of them:

- Cameras and microphones are used to record visual and audio information in real situations with real people, as opposed to actors in studios. This audio-visual material ranges from wide overviews and background sounds to close-ups and intimate proximity to the people being recorded. Often, cameras and microphones are hand-held, giving the impression that real situations are unfolding as opposed to being set up.
- The *mise-en-scène* shows us actual places and events. The people in documentaries are known as social actors and can include participants who are the central subject of the documentary, other participants or eye witnesses and experts. Lighting and sound quality are likely to be poorer than for fictional texts,

which will usually signify the authenticity of the documentary. The documentary may also use archive footage and interviews, images of newspaper headlines, maps and diagrams to explain certain things.
- Non-diegetic music will often be used to evoke certain feelings or emotions.

The way in which the above elements are constructed into a narrative is key to understanding the form of documentary. As with news media, it is easy for a documentary text to be accepted by the audience as showing things just as they are. However, the different recorded aspects of real situations are selected and composed together in the editing process to construct an apparently seamless narrative. This means that certain things are included while others are excluded. What is included is arranged in a specific order that usually represents a version of reality from one particular perspective. This is then used to support a particular argument or point of view. The process is further emphasised by the use of the presenter and/or voice-over (whose commentary can seem to have the authority of the 'voice of God'), as well as the use of written titles to direct the audience. This process is designed to prompt the audience to a **preferred reading** of what they see and hear, so the audience will agree with the documentary producer's viewpoint.

Anvil! The Story of Anvil

This is a feature-length documentary that was initially shown in smaller independent and art-house cinemas. It follows the lives of two leading members of a Canadian heavy metal band who are now in their 50s, but have not given up on being rock musicians, despite the fact that they still haven't made it, and have to carry out fairly menial jobs in order to survive and support their families.

It is hard to consider this film without reference to the mockumentary This is Spinal Tap. Spinal Tap also followed the fortunes and misfortunes of a rock band and used the forms of documentary, but was entirely fictitious, using actors and scripting to create a comedy about a deluded band.

Anvil makes knowing reference to Spinal Tap, and constructs some great comic moments by setting up audience expectations and then thwarting them. However, overall the documentary invites the audience to take a much more sympathetic view of the subjects. Instead of representing the two as sad middle-aged men who should have grown up and got sensible jobs a long time ago, the documentary positions the viewer to see them as determined and heroic, and we want them to succeed.

There is a noticeable lack of voice-over or presenter in the documentary, although the audience is guided by the use of titles. This could lead us to see the documentary as being observational or even interactive/cinéma vérité, although the way that it has been edited and shaped into a very clear narrative suggests more of an expositional piece.

His Infernal Majesty

Radio 1's documentary on the Finnish band His Infernal Majesty (HIM) presents similar content to Anvil by looking at a heavy metal band. Both documentaries use interviews with experts in the form of members of successful bands of the same genre who discuss the subjects. However, in the *Anvil* documentary this is used to emphasise Anvil's fall into obscurity after having some initial success and influence in the 1980s, whereas the *HIM* documentary continues to use commentaries from contemporaries all the way through to signify that they are well established.

Radio documentaries can use microphones and audio description to create images of real situations as effectively as a camera could. However, the *HIM* documentary has almost no 'actuality' recording, and instead relies almost entirely on interviews intercut with voice-over presentation, backed by music from the band, to create the text. This is a more expository approach, where the interviewees support the thrust of the voice-over in presenting the band as something of a novelty, as they become a success in this musical genre despite coming from Helsinki.

The scheduling of the documentary on Radio 1 during a weekday evening and the fairly straightforward linear narrative following HIM from obscurity to success, with lots of factual information thrown in, suggests that this documentary is aimed at fans of the genre, and more specifically at fans of the band. This again is in contrast to the *Anvil* documentary, which will probably be of interest to metal fans, but tells a far more universal human story through themes of struggle, determination, failure and growing older that has much wider appeal.

'Reality TV': a hybrid of documentary form

The term 'reality TV' suggests a strong connection to documentary, and as such can be considered a hybrid of the form. As we have already seen with the codes and conventions of documentary making, the notion that we should accept we are seeing and hearing objective reality needs to be questioned in our analysis. This is also a recommended approach to take with the representations made in 'reality TV'.

As with documentary form, taking a historical perspective on the development of 'reality TV' will give us a good idea of the various forms of the genre, and how they have developed.

One of the threads of 'reality TV' comes from a documentary TV series from the 1970s called *An American Family* which used *cinéma-verité*/fly-on-the-wall observational techniques over an extended period of time to document the life of one family. This format was transferred to a British series that did the same thing. This idea of observing specific groups of people over an extended series, rather than as a one-off documentary, began to spread to include series like *COPS* and led to the BBC's first run of the series *Airport* in the 1990s. Meanwhile, another innovation was the 'fish-out-of-water' approach, where real people were filmed being put into unfamiliar contexts and the audience saw what they would do and how they would interact, for instance MTV's *The Real World*. In 1997, Swedish TV broadcast *Expedition Robinson*, and the concept was franchised around the world as *Survivor*. This show extended the fish-out-of-water idea into 'strangers isolated together in a strange environment'. Most importantly, it combined documentary codes and conventions with game show forms, such as competition and elimination over a series of weeks. By the time Dutch TV company Endemol launched the first *Big Brother* in 1999, 'reality TV' was becoming a recognised genre with the two distinctive strands showing:

- peoples' lives being observed over a series
- people being isolated and observed in a challenging, unfamiliar environment

The Apprentice

The Apprentice fits in with the latter format, where a group of professionals compete through a number of challenges over a series of weeks for a real job with successful businessman, Sir Alan Sugar. It is interesting to note from an institutional point of view that *The Apprentice* was created by Mark Burnett, a UK TV producer who had sold the *Survivor* franchise to American TV.

Use of forms

The Apprentice utilises recognisable forms of documentary such as:

- hand-held cameras and microphones
- observation of events as they unfold
- use of interviews
- non-diegetic music for dramatic and emotional effect
- use of voice-over

However, the narrative is driven by the competitive game show format, with the voice-over constantly reminding us of the aim of the programme and shots being selected and constructed through the editing to support this. The resulting seamless juxtapositions of close-ups and reaction shots show the body language of stress, conflict, victory and failure.

Representation

Representation in *The Apprentice* reveals a number of things. The range of gender, ethnicity, nationality, culture and socio-economic backgrounds in the participants suggests that this is an example of the BBC's public-service remit having some effect. The programme may support a very capitalist idea of a 'survival-of-the-fittest' environment where the desire for a six-figure salary is the motivating force, but it wants to offer this to as big a demographic range as it can get from 12 people. The show is also somewhat like *Anvil* in its positive representation of older people, where the boss and his assistants are close to retirement age and use experience and wisdom to choose the best of the young participants, who tend to be portrayed as being a arrogant, naive and out of their depth.

Audience

There are a number of gratifications for the audience in watching a show of this nature. There is the satisfaction of knowing the format (the generic and narrative conventions), but having to guess or anticipate how each episode, and the whole series, will finally be resolved. The audience can also be voyeuristic, being able to observe what happens to the participants without being challenged and getting pleasure from seeing other people's suffering and distress. Media analyst Tom

Alderman questions the audience's interest in wanting to watch this when he suggests that 'there is a sub-set of "reality TV" that can only be described as shame TV because it uses humiliation as its core appeal'.

The internet as a second platform

The use of the internet as a second media platform for the documentary and hybrid forms topic is similar to its use in the broadcast or film fiction option. Like *The Archers*, *The Apprentice* has its own dedicated section of web pages on **www.bbc.co.uk**, where the audience can catch up on episodes, read more information about each contestant and participate on the message board, nicknamed 'the Watercooler' — a metaphor for the place in offices where people gather and gossip. There is also The Predictor, where you can interact live online as the programme is broadcast with a device that allows you to predict who will be fired. The Predictor also lets the player see what other participants are predicting and it awards points at the end of the show. This is a very good example of two platforms being utilised simultaneously by the audience.

This cross-platform usage is also possible for radio listeners. They could be listening to a Radio 1 music documentary on the BBC iPlayer while browsing through the relevant Radio 1 pages on **www.bbc.co.uk**, so incorporating text and images to their audio experience. Audio, whether music or speech, lends itself particularly well to web-based multi-tasking, as the sound can continue in the background while the listener browses and interacts with multiple sites.

The internet hosts a lot of unofficial websites that generate content based on *The Apprentice*. There are *Apprentice*-related blogs and message boards on sites for professionals such as lawyers and business managers, which reveal how popular the show is with the business community. There are also sites that show user-generated content like the Lego Apprentice (which also features on YouTube). Each week, the makers, known as the Boleg Bros, take the soundtrack from the original programme and re-edit the dialogue to visuals using Lego figures to create a spoof version of the show. For some people, there is as much anticipation and pleasure gained from the Lego version as there is from the original, although the satire only works in relation to the broadcast show.

Print as a platform

Print as a platform for the extension of the documentary and hybrid texts also has similarities to the way that broadcast or film fiction is treated. *The Anvil* documentary as a feature-length theatrical cinema release documentary would be considered good content for film magazines. Given the subject matter of the metal music genre, it would also provide material for music magazines like *Kerrang!* or *Metal Hammer*.

Like other blockbuster 'reality TV' and game shows, such as the *X Factor*, or *Big Brother*, *The Apprentice* provides plenty of material for newspapers, particularly the tabloids. The red-top papers, such as the *Sun* and the *Mirror*, use conflicts between the show's participants to whip up a frenzy of gossip and polarisation because they know that it will help sell their papers. The representations and constructions of conflict between apparently difficult characters, which the selection and editing of content guidance

the programme produces, is taken on board by the tabloids and magnified further, producing grotesque stereotypes for the pleasure of the audience.

As we have seen, print is also a part of the BBC's own offering, and *The Apprentice* is a key feature of *Radio Times* when the series is showing. During the 12-week run of the 2008 show, Sir Alan Sugar appeared on the front cover of *Radio Times* twice, revealing the importance of the show to the BBC as a ratings winner.

Extension broadcasts

With a high-audience-rating programme like *The Apprentice*, the BBC maximises extension and coverage across all of its media platforms and services. The broadcast itself is directly followed by another broadcast, *The Apprentice: You're Fired!,* which instantly continues the narrative through a studio-based panel/chat show where the most recently fired apprentice is interviewed by the presenter, Adrian Chiles. Although the original programme has been pre-recorded some months earlier, the scheduling of the two shows one after the other appears to produce a seamless narrative for the viewer.

The coverage is furthered by a regular interview slot for the sacked contestant the next morning on BBC Radio 5 Live, as well as appearances on breakfast TV shows and the homepage of **www.bbc.co.uk**.

Topic 3: lifestyle

Growth in popularity of lifestyle texts

Lifestyle issues such as home and fashion make-overs, slimming and child rearing have been part of the offering of magazines for decades, as can be seen with titles such as *Woman* and *Woman's Own*. The 1990s saw a big increase in the popularity of all genres of magazines (nearly a 60% rise between 1994 and 1999), but especially those dealing with different lifestyle topics such as *Practical Parenting* or the publication *Psychologies,* which gives psychological and behavioural issues a distinctly glamorous spin.

The increase in the number of broadcast channels, which we have already explored, has also led to more scheduling of lifestyle programming. In the late 1990s the term '**masthead television**' was used to describe the way that magazine titles began to expand into TV, with titles like *Good Housekeeping* providing programmes for Sky. Lifestyle programming has expanded to give viewers whole channels devoted to lifestyle issues, such as Living. Meanwhile, on terrestrial TV, lifestyle strands have popped up with increasing regularity as part of daytime offerings, and particularly on Channel 4, right through and beyond the watershed, with cookery and property make-over shows like *Grand Designs*, to Gok Wan's more daring *How to Look Good Naked*.

Lifestyle productions for all media platforms are popular with producers because they are generally relatively cheap to produce. For example, because Channel 4 is a publisher broadcaster (see the Glossary), lifestyle programming makes good sense, since these sorts of programmes keep commissioning costs low. Lifestyle content also allows for the promotion of a range of products and services, so it is popular with advertisers and the producers of related lifestyle products and services, such as clothing and dietary courses.

The internet as a platform

The comparative ease with which websites can be set up means that the internet can provide highly targeted lifestyle sites. It is important to cover the relationship of this topic to advertising and marketing theory, along with an analysis of a range of lifestyle texts using the key concepts.

As well as seeing the creation of spin-off publications and websites from broadcast lifestyle shows, for instance **www.trinnyandsusannah.com**, there are also cases where older lifestyle magazines have taken on the internet, and produced relatively simple audio-visual content for their sites, for example like Cosmo TV from *Cosmopolitan* magazine.

Lifestyle content and gaming

Gaming, and especially online gaming, is emerging as an area where lifestyle content is taking off. Massively Multiplayer Online Role Playing Games (MMORPGs) are often associated with fantasy worlds, like World of Warcraft. However, particularly for older users, virtual reality RPGs that are more similar to the real world, such as Second Life and There, are also becoming popular. Real-world businesses are creating a presence in these games as a way of extending marketing possibilities for real-world products. Second Life has virtual stores for lifestyle companies and brands like Adidas, Reebok, Calvin Klein and Kraft.

Through creating avatar characters that need clothing and houses that need furnishing, users try out lifestyle choices in the virtual environment before doing the same in the real world. However, real-world companies using Second Life to promote and sell their actual products (it is estimated that transactions worth around $1.5million are carried out everyday via Second Life) are finding that the game is also being used by people to sell fake copies of branded goods.

The Sims is a virtual world RPG that used to have an online version, but closed it down. This could be seen as a safer option for businesses. On The Sims website there is a store where you can purchase home décor, DIY, clothing and hair products to use in the game. One of these is a game extra called Ikea Home Stuff, which provides furniture items for Sims houses based on real Ikea products. There is a similar opportunity to go to a virtual H&M shop and buy clothing. In this offline version, the businesses are still providing content that will help to market real-world products without the threat of piracy.

Audience and representation

The link between audience and representation in lifestyle texts is very strong. The audience is looking to the texts to improve and add to their existing lives, so they want to see and read about people like them. However, they don't simply want their lives reflected, they also want something to aspire to, so producers need to make their representations not only relevant and accessible to their audiences, but also inspirational.

Traditionally, the audience for lifestyle texts has tended to be associated with female and family interests. However, one of the impacts of the 90s' boom in lifestyle magazines was the rise in titles for men. Although some of these were described as 'lads' mags' and contained little more than soft porn, there were also titles that dealt with health and fashion for men.

Many lifestyle texts also have content that appeals to an ageing population. As people are living longer and the baby boomers are reaching retirement age, media producers and advertisers are targeting more products at the older audience.

Topic 4: music

In a case study on this topic, the following are areas that you could consider.

- With the advent of downloads and other technological developments, your study will incorporate a range of platforms including music magazines and fan websites as well as specialist music radio and television channels. The niche marketing of music through specialist magazines such as *The Platform,* a Muslim hip hop title, and internet radio stations like **www.rastaites.com** catering for fans of the reggae genre, should also be explored.
- Analysis of the way that music is covered more generally as a subject in other areas of the media would be useful, for instance in newspaper articles, colour supplements and television interviews, as well as in merchandising and tie-ins such as film theme tunes. Marketing theory is especially relevant here, as is analysing texts using the key concepts.
- The impact of new media technology on both audiences and music producers is an essential study area. The landscape of the music industry has changed drastically since the end of the 90s, when the industry's revenue sources from selling recorded music started to dry up as fans began to share and download MP3 files for free. As bands like Radiohead ditch their major record labels and distribute their own music via the internet, and mainstream acts give away their latest CDs in Sunday magazines, your case study should explore the role that different media platforms play in the process.
- Another approach to this topic might be to look at the impact that major media events have on the music industry. This could range from the *X Factor*'s dominance of the pop charts, through acts that are manufactured before our very eyes, to the BBC's multi-platform coverage of Glastonbury.
- Representation could be covered effectively by looking at the way different media platforms give access to music that appeals to different ethnic, social or gender demographics. This might, for example, involve investigating the way that digital technology has enabled the BBC to offer many more stations nationally that can provide the highly specific content that used to only be broadcast on city-based stations and urban pirate radio.

Topic 5: news

This topic is concerned with how news is presented across media platforms. News production is a hugely important aspect of media, and you should look into key ideas that have been developed about this.

- Key theories include the idea of **gatekeeping,** along with **Galtung and Ruge's identification of news values** such as prominence, proximity, timeliness and human interest. Perhaps the most important consideration will be how the news represents people, places, issues and ideas and whether the mediated version of reality presented by the news journalist (whether radio, television, print or e-media) can ever represent the reality of the event objectively, without taking a particular perspective. This would lead to consideration of journalistic styles and the use of Barthes' theories of anchorage and cropping of images in print and web media.
- With the increase in interactive media, you may well consider the relationship between the audience and institution in contributing to, and determining, how the news is selected and presented. For example, you could examine the relationship between the news and public relations, and the role of 'spin doctors' in the presentation of politicians and celebrities. Another possible area of debate would be the 'dumbing down' of news and the increase in 'infotainment', particularly in the print and e-media platforms.
- Another key issue for cross-platform study is the way that internet news is threatening to kill off print news altogether, because it is free and constantly updated. Younger audiences are moving away from newspapers and consequently advertising revenues are suffering. Traditional newspapers, from the *Sun* to the *Guardian,* are having to become digital news providers. This puts them in direct competition with broadcasters, such as the BBC. In addition, none of the newspaper producers has found an effective model for funding online news provision.
- The development of blogs and podcasts and opportunities for audiences to respond as citizen journalists (with the suggestion that news reporting has become more democratic) is also an important area of research.

Topic 6: sport

The way in which sport is represented and promoted on different media platforms should be the focus of your case study.

- You could explore the development of the sportsperson as celebrity, for instance among premiership footballers or top-seeded women tennis players, and the overlap between these and other celebrities such as film and TV stars and musicians.
- The ways in which sports have become professionalised, and the impact of media revenue, are central issues to this topic.
- The role of advertising and marketing and convergence of media to promote the sport and associated products is also very important. Football clubs, for

example, have become brands used to promote themselves and other products. Merchandising, PR sponsorship and product placement are evident in the development of sport across a range of platforms including specialist magazines, websites and television channels dedicated to sport — even to specific football clubs.

- The impact of satellite channels, especially Sky, in the shift away from traditional screening of sports programmes can be discussed.
- The development of interactive television, which gives the audience a range of features enabling them to gain some control over how they watch sports programmes, is a significant development of the technology.
- Segmentation and packaging of audiences through TV channels, specialist magazines, sports supplements and the placement of sports coverage in newspapers is also important.

Marketing, advertising and the media

Marketing and advertising is not examined as a topic, but it is considered an essential area of study for media students.

Matching target audiences

The purpose of marketing is to persuade a target audience to buy and use products and services.

In order to get the messages across, advertisers need to use media platforms, because these are specifically designed to reach massive audiences. We have already referred to the idea of media producers creating media texts for target audiences. Essentially, media producers and advertisers do the same thing — they try to communicate with a target audience — but for different purposes.

For example, Channel 4's *How to Look Good Naked* targets a range of women, between teenagers and fifty-year-olds. These women are likely to be a mixture of middle and working class, from all regions of the UK, and from most ethnic backgrounds. They will all share an interest in body awareness — weight, make-up, hair and fashion. This is a demographic description of the target audience for the programme.

Meanwhile, in the world of commerce, there are manufacturers of products and services aimed at exactly the same target group. These include hair-care and beauty products, fashionable clothes and services like Weight Watchers. These manufacturers will work with marketing companies to produce adverts that can be broadcast immediately before, during and after the programme.

What we have here is a 'match' of target audiences. Channel 4 is happy because it brings in advertising revenue. This allows the channel to exist, because it does not receive a licence fee as the BBC does, neither does it get subscriptions like satellite and cable TV companies. The advertisers and manufacturers are happy because they have reached millions of people who fit the demographic they are targeting.

Marketing theory

As well as the match concept, other aspects of marketing and advertising link to the media.

The terminology

The word '**market**' began as a noun to describe a physical space where provisions and livestock are sold. As industrialisation and fragmentation of the population took place, 'markets' became less connected with physical space and more of an abstract idea. The 'market' for a certain type of product or service now means the demand for those products, regardless of where the buyers may be located, like 'the financial markets' or 'the black market'. As a result, the verb 'to market' describes the act of promoting products and services to dispersed markets. Different media platforms are very good at attracting particular demographic groupings that are not physically located in the same place.

'**Branding**' also has old agricultural roots, meaning 'burning' and was used to describe burning the name or symbol of an owner on to livestock. Its modern use has the same idea; a brand tells us who owns or manufactures a product.

Role of marketing and advertising

Advertising and marketing are essential aspects of capitalist economies, where trade and industry are mainly controlled by private companies for profit. Huge amounts are spent on marketing, in particular on branding and advertising, as part of the profit-making process. Because of the expectations of advertising, non-profit-making organisations such as the health service or charities employ similar tactics.

Branding and advertising aim to provide two essentials: trust and value. The customers, or audience, buy brands because they trust the product or service. Advertising no longer simply announces the availability of something — it sells us a set of values. Adverts appeal to us by suggesting that we will have a particular lifestyle through owning the product or using the service. We might take notice of an advert for a BMW car not just because we need transport, but because we trust the reliability of the brand, and because we might think it will make us appear sophisticated and wealthy. The brand and the advertising send out the message that the product has value far beyond its function.

Questions
&
Answers

In this part of the guide we will look at some answers to example texts and questions. These will be followed by examiner's comments, indicated by the symbol *e*, which will explain why the answers have received certain grades. This will give you a clear insight into what examiners are looking for in student responses to the AS exam.

For the unseen text in Section A we will be analysing a website homepage that you will find in Appendix 1 to this guide. In Section B we will be looking at questions and answers that cover the four media concepts of forms, representation, institutions and audience, each of which will use a different case study example.

Section A example text: music website

See Appendix 1 (p. 76) for the picture of the website page. The text that accompanies the picture is given below:

> Leipzig Zoo is an indie band signed to the Tough Rade label, which started in the late 1970s as an independent music label promoting the work of post-punk and indie rock bands, including The Smits, and more recently The Stokes, The Arcades and Babyshams.
>
> Leipzig Zoo has risen to prominence through its involvement with BBC Introducing, which is the brand name for new music showcased across the BBC network, from Radio 1's *New Black Music Show* to *Raw Talent* on local BBC Radio Humberside. BBC Introducing also hosts stages at Glastonbury and other major festivals that previously would have carried the Radio 1 branding.

Question 1: media forms

How does the website homepage use conventional media forms to appeal to the audience?

Candidates' responses to Question 1

A-grade answer

The website uses conventional forms, despite having a unique artistic style that makes it appear different from other websites. The page uses a combination of images, words and layout features to make it attractive to the viewer. It has a name, like a headline, which we assume is the band's name. It is the biggest text and it is angled across an image of five people, presumably the band. The name uses unusual typography with a capital 'Z' in the middle of the first word, matching the 'Z' in the second word, which makes it stand out. The non-serif font gives a contemporary feel, although the body text looks a bit like old typewriter text.

The image of the group is somewhere between a photo and a drawing, and like the typography, suggests the arty indie genre of the group. Viewers will expect to see a picture of the band because it gives a good sense of what they look like, their visual style and how it relates to the genre. The group is looking out because this is a way of engaging the viewer.

The navigation bar uses terms like 'home', 'news' and 'blog' that we tend to see on most websites. We expect these will hyperlink to other parts of the site.

The top right has a banner headline for a phone company, with its easily recognised logo. Other logos, such as for downloading music and services, and for social networking, don't have any text to explain them. They do not need to because they do what logos should do, which is to communicate instantly the brand and all the associations that go with it.

Top left is the record company logo with a picture to the right which is probably a thumbnail of the new CD cover. The monkey image on the CD is echoed as the background layer of the page to reinforce this visual feature that will be associated with the new release. Below this are details for fans about the CD and about the band's tour of festivals.

The bottom right has video and sound players and a photo download. The audience would be familiar with the symbols for playing and pausing content, because they will probably have seen these things on sites like YouTube.

We can see that the website uses generic conventions that users would recognise from experiencing other websites, and that it is non-linear, which means the viewer can choose how they navigate around the site.

> The answer clearly describes a variety of the conventions used in detail. It shows very clear understanding of the purposes of different parts of the page, and the expectations and assumptions that users will have of it. The answer constantly refers to the website and uses plenty of appropriate media terminology with confidence. It widens the discussion from what we see to include, for instance, the explanation of the way logos and branding work.

C-grade answer

This website uses lots of conventions that you find on other websites, especially for music. The site is for a band with a bit of a strange name, which makes them look and sound like they are probably an indie band. You can tell the name of the band because it is the biggest writing on the web page. This lets the viewer know what they are looking at, so they don't get confused. There is also a picture of the band itself, so the viewer can see what they look like.

The web page has a bar with the names of other pages, like 'home', 'news' and 'blog'. This bar shows the user where to connect to other pages on the website. There are things like a video player on the website for watching the band, and a way of listening to their music and downloading their photos, which will probably be good for fans of the band. You see these sorts of things on lots of music websites.

There is quite a lot of written information, such as the tour dates of the band, and some things about their new album. There is a quote from a music magazine which says that the band is 'the best sound' so far this year, which means that the magazine's journalists must think they are very good.

There are also symbols for different internet sites, like social network and music download sites that are connected to this band, and fans can connect to these sites from this homepage.

So, a lot of the things that we can see on this homepage are the sorts of things that music fans would expect to see and know how to use.

🖉 This answer shows some satisfactory knowledge and understanding of how the web page uses generic conventions, but in some places it is quite basic. Although it covers quite a lot of information, it is far more descriptive than the A-grade piece, and does not use much effective, detailed media language. For example, the candidate describes the navigation bar as just a bar and there is a lack of detail about the fonts being used. The answer concentrates on describing what is seen on the page and does not attempt to explain or discuss how the page uses conventions with reference to other ideas.

■ ■ ■

Question 2: media representation

Consider the representations of people on the website homepage.

Candidates' responses to Question 2

A-grade answer

There are five people represented. The main image, a manipulated photo, seems to be designed to make them look interesting. They appear young, either in their late teens or early twenties. The two males at the back on the right are, perhaps, a little older. Only one is female. They all seem to be white, although the male on the left looks like he could be of Asian origin. Overall this reflects the impression that the indie genre of music probably appeals mostly, but not exclusively, to a white audience. This is different from other genres such as R and B, or Dubstep, which tend to appeal to a wider demographic.

The female band member seems to stand out more. Unlike the others there is a close-up image of her in the thumbnails. She seems to be the singer in the video clip, and looks like she is the visual focus of the group.

They are dressed casually and some look a bit nerdy, it is almost a stereotype because it suggests that appearance does not matter; it's the music that counts. This may be why they look so serious in the main image. They have been positioned to look out at the viewer, almost challenging us to make eye contact with them. Even the background image of the mask-like monkey, with its dark eyes, looks intense.

Although the seriousness dominates, some of the download picture thumbnails suggest more that they are having fun, and the CD album uses a play on words, which suggests there is a humorous side to them. The YouTube player shows the group playing in a concert at Glastonbury, and this gives them a sense of authenticity and credibility in the same way that the music magazine quote does.

The band has a German-sounding name, which adds to the European arty, alternative feel of the way the website looks, and seems well designed to fit with the genre.

It could also signify a kind of intellectual elitism. However, the site has a US tour date, and that could suggest that they are looking for, and starting to get, more mainstream success by breaking into the lucrative American market. This is echoed by their connection to mainstream brands shown in the logos, including allowing a major phone company to advertise. Most of the logos represent brands that appeal to a younger mainstream audience.

> The answer refers effectively to what can be observed on the homepage, and then moves on to explain possible reasons for the representations. The way in which this is written shows the candidate clearly understands that the site has been constructed deliberately to appear in a certain way, to give a certain impression. As well as considering the demographic from the visual information, the answer extends ideas about representation by discussing the way in which the written text reinforces and adds to the visuals.

C-grade answer

There are five people shown in the main picture on this website, and these same five people also appear in the smaller pictures below, showing them on a YouTube-type clip in concert and also mucking about in a studio. The way that they are dressed has a stereotypically indie look to it. They are all dressed in quite ordinary clothes, and they don't appear to have made much effort to look glamorous. This is a reflection of the genre of music, so it helps people to recognise what sort of music is being promoted on this website.

They are young people, which is what you would expect in a band. There is a mixture of male and female, but mainly male and this could tell us that this band is more for males than females. The male on the left looks as though he could be from a Chinese or Japanese ethnic background, whereas the other members of the band look like white Europeans.

In the main picture, the people in the band have had some sort of computer effect put on them to make it look as though this is a drawing, although you can still see that they are in a photo. This makes them look more interesting, which will make the audience think that they are not just an ordinary band.

The smaller pictures show them mucking about and having a laugh, which shows the viewer that they are also a fun band. This makes them look as though they are probably good to watch live.

> This answer shows understanding of what representation is. It describes what can be seen in the images, and in some cases attempts to explain what the pictures are trying to convey to the viewer. Although the answer shows that a variety of representational issues has been noticed, such as age, gender and ethnicity, there has not been much attempt to explain why these things have been done in this way, or what they are attempting to convey to the audience. This response shows that the writer has some understanding of issues covered

in media studies, but they have used very little effective and accurate specialist vocabulary, and the analysis barely goes beyond description.

■ ■ ■

Question 3: media institutions

In what ways does the website connect across different media platforms to a range of different media producers?

Candidates' responses to Question 3

A-grade answer

The webpage connects to the music industry, broadcast radio and TV, and new media. It is a good example of media synergy; the promotion of the band brings together a variety of media products, services and platforms through the brand logo links.

Several institutions represent the music industry. A well-established label features next to the CD, emphasising who the band are with. This company will probably have suffered from illegal downloading, so they offer various formats to buy. There is a link to a well-known music site, so people can download legitimately. This also allows Leipzig Zoo's label to by-pass dealing with major record companies, like Universal, to distribute their recordings.

The music industry is further represented by tour dates at major festivals, with a link to a ticketing service that is another trusted brand fans will recognise. This connects to the illegal download issue, because record companies are looking to make money from concerts rather than relying on shrinking sales of recordings.

The BBC bridges music and broadcast. Radio 1 has long been important for music promotion. BBC Presenting clarifies this role. It probably also supports the corporation fulfilling its public service remit, because it supports a range of music from many genres and diverse minority groups right across its local and national services. One of the biggest music magazines is also referred to, and their opinion is obviously valued by the band and record label.

Finally, the website also has links to other new media institutions. The social networking sites referred to encourage communication between the band and its fans. YouTube is a more democratic form of broadcasting than the BBC, allowing fans to see specific clips of the band when they want. The radio station that is mentioned will do a similar thing, making it easy to listen to tracks of the band. The advert for the smart phone also makes sense, promoting a product that converges many of the new media that fans could use.

✏ This answer starts with a clear statement of the platforms and industries covered, and then goes on to be absolutely specific about the evidence for this within the web page, rather than making generalisations. It usefully groups the different institutions and shows how the brands link out to specific platforms. It makes very good use of the contextual information accompanying the question, and links this effectively with other evidence. It explains how the advert has been placed on the site for good reason. In addition, the answer shows wider knowledge and understanding of issues facing the music industry, and this knowledge is used to explain why certain things are included on the homepage. The answer effectively applies relevant media terms such as 'synergy'.

C-grade answer

The homepage has lots of connections to different media platforms, like the BBC and social networking sites. You can click on the different links for each of the different organisations and these will take you to each of the companies shown on the webpage. For example you could click on the link to the ticketing service and that will take you to their website to buy tickets for Leipzig Zoo's concerts. In some ways this is good for fans because it means that it makes it easy for them to find out about buying tickets for the band's gigs. However, it could be that the fans could buy tickets more cheaply from another place, and they might not think about that.

There is also a link to a major music downloading site. This gives the fans a good opportunity to download the band's music straight away, without having to go to a shop, or order a CD from somewhere like HMV. Having this link makes things convenient.

The biggest institution is probably the BBC. Mentioning the BBC, and having a link to the Glastonbury festival footage, will make people viewing the site think that Leipzig Zoo are getting well known, because they can see that a major media producer has recognised them. This is a bit similar to Leipzig Zoo's record label that is mentioned. If the viewer knows about the label and the bands that have been on it, they will immediately think that Leipzig Zoo is an indie band, associated with the famous groups already on this label, like The Stokes.

So the way that the website is able to connect to other platforms makes things easier for the fans and makes the band look well established.

> Some useful points are made in the answer, showing understanding of how the web page connects to other platforms. Overall, however, most of what is said could be worked out by anyone who has some experience of using such a website. This is because the focus of the answer is really on the user, or fan, and how they see and interact with media institutions. This can be contrasted with the A-grade response, which concentrates more on how different media organisations themselves utilise the web to make connections across media platforms. Candidate B's answer does use some of the contextual information that has been provided by the exam board. However, this question on media industries is probably where candidates should make substantial use of this added information. There could be better use of specific media terminology about media institutions, rather than general descriptions. There is also a sense

that the answer meanders between ideas, as opposed to being organised into clear ideas and points.

■ ■ ■

Question 4: media audience

In what ways does the website appeal to a general target audience and specifically to fans of the group?

Candidates' responses to Question 4

A-grade answer

Because music is about identity, the target audience will probably reflect aspects of the band's appearance. They are likely to be young and male, although the female may attract other females, much like Florence and the Machine would do. The indie genre is likely to attract a mainly white, middle- to lower-middle-class audience, who may have stayed on at school or have been university students. The concert dates suggest a fan base that is mainly UK based, but there is also an appeal to a North American audience.

The visual and graphic style will also be appealing. The strong contrasting colours, the images of the band and the background image of the monkey are given an artistic treatment that goes beyond what a straightforward mainstream pop act might use. There is something serious and brooding about the band and the other visuals, suggesting something about the lifestyle that could attract the audience. This may also be shown by the gigs advertised — festivals rather than urban concerts, appealing to people who are willing to travel beyond towns and cities. The use of the music magazine quote reinforces the type of fans being addressed, because this publication tends to cover certain genres including indie music, and certainly other bands that this label has produced.

There is plenty on the site for fans and aficionados. The video and audio players, photo downloads, members' area and forums are all added extras designed to be gratifying to more than just the casual listener and viewer. The YouTube link also allows for the possibility of serious fans creating user-generated material by filming gigs with their mobile phones and then editing and uploading them to share with other fans.

The amount of reference on the site to new digital media providers tells us that the site is attracting digital natives — young people immersed in new media, who are likely to be early adopters of media innovations, using these for their own pleasure, hence the advert for the smart phone.

> 🖉 The answer starts with a detailed demographic description of the target audience, which is given some justification and explanation. Having done this, the references to what appeals to the target group make more sense because

the audience has been defined. A variety of features of the homepage and their appeal are discussed in depth. As well as demographic descriptors, the answer uses other effective media language to discuss audiences, for example the terms used to describe fan types, and reference to the gratifications and uses of this text for the audience. The users are seen as active participators and generators of content; their fluency with media technology is well considered.

C-grade answer

The general target audience will probably be people who like indie-type music. This group is usually aged about 14 upwards to people in their twenties, or even thirties. It is quite male oriented, although quite a lot of females like this sort of music too.

The website looks like it is for indie fans, mainly through the way that the band look, which is quite serious and casually dressed. This will appeal because the audience for this sort of music probably look and dress in a similar way.

If you were someone who knew a bit about this band, then the website would be a useful place to look to find out about new releases and gigs, which is exactly what this page does, so that is why the target audience would be attracted to the site. Also they might want to find out some more background information about the band, and they could get that too.

If you were a proper fan of the group, the website would be good for the same reasons as above, but for other things too. The site has videos and photos of the band, and this is the sort of thing that fans of groups want to see. They can also hear the latest singles and download the new album from the website.

The other thing that this homepage gives to fans of the group is a members' area. This wouldn't be so interesting to people who weren't fans, because it would have information and stuff especially for fans who were really into the band, like biography details and the latest information that would only be interesting if you really liked the group.

> This response gives some consideration to who might be interested in the website, either as a casual observer, or as a fan. The description of the audience covers age and gender, but it does not attempt to give any more demographic detail, such as level of education, lifestyle or location of the target audience. Some connections are made between the content and style of the site and the lifestyle and appearance of the audience. Distinctions are made between the casual and more hardcore user, and how certain features will appeal to the different level of audience. These distinctions are fairly simple and they are not discussed in much detail. Many features of the site that are designed to appeal have not been addressed.

■ ■ ■

Section B cross-media study: sample answers

Question 1: media forms

Account for the similarities and differences in the codes and conventions used in the media products from your case study.

Candidates' responses to Question 1

The candidates' answers to this question use a documentary and hybrid forms case study.

A-grade answer

My case study is on documentary and hybrid forms. I will be using three example texts from three platforms: the feature-length film documentary *Anvil! The Story of Anvil*, a Radio 1 documentary *His Infernal Majesty* (*HIM*) on the band of the same name, and the BBC 1 'reality TV' programme *The Apprentice*. I will compare similarities and differences in the format of these texts in their initial broadcast/cinema platforms, and then look at their treatment on the web and in print.

> 🖉 The introduction clearly indicates the main platform, the example texts and the other platforms covered.

All three texts use recognisable documentary conventions to signify to the audience that they are about objective reality, rather than fictional texts. The two moving image texts use techniques to establish a sense of observed reality that can be traced back to the earliest documentarists such as Flaherty and Grierson. The *mise-en-scène* in *Anvil* and *The Apprentice* portray places that we believe actually exist, from Canadian shopping centres to the City of London. The use of hand-held cameras, close-ups, wide shots and on-camera sound are technical codes that lead the audience to think that what we hear and see is authentically based on reality. The Radio 1 documentary lacks any attempt to set a realistic context, and is structured around a set of studio interviews and links. It could be argued that this is because it is a radio documentary. However, there are many radio documentaries, particularly on Radio 4, that use 'field' recordings to give a sense of the reality of a place.

> 🖉 The first main paragraph sets up high expectations of this candidate because there is detailed and fluent use of technical and media vocabulary, such as 'close-ups', 'wide shots', 'signify' and 'technical codes' to support ideas. The candidate very clearly understands what is meant by 'media forms' because they are effectively discussing the various codes and conventions used in documentary. References to the supporting examples are fully embedded in the discussion, and these are used to compare in detail how each text uses the

forms of documentary. This section also shows an understanding of historical context by reference to the initiators of the documentary form.

All three texts use non-diegetic music in a similar way, to add emotion and feeling to the visuals. With *HIM* this is not much more than using the band's music as a backdrop. *The Apprentice* on the other hand has a set of themes that it uses throughout the series, from classical music to signify the gravitas and drama of big business in the city, to an urgent contemporary track indicating when someone will be fired.

This paragraph develops the first by adding relevant knowledge and understanding of documentary forms, with a clear idea of the purpose of non-diegetic music shown through direct reference to the example texts.

Anvil is the text that sticks with a more objective view, using a *cinéma verité* style which seems to allow the audience to make up its mind about what is unfolding. This is helped by the lack of a voice-over (VO), which in the other two texts is used as an authoritative 'voice of God', making them more expository by providing guidance as to how the audience should make sense of the text. However, *Anvil* does still guide the audience — all three texts have selected the recordings and composed them in a way that is designed to lead the audience to a preferred reading.

Here the candidate shows a sophisticated understanding of the form by reference to a particular documentary movement and subsequently to different sub-genres of documentary such as observational and expository styles, as well as by reference to the key audience theory of types of 'readings'.

The Apprentice is a hybrid with a game-show narrative — it has competitive tasks with winners and losers. This is clear in the narrative structure that the voice-over keeps reminding us of. With *Anvil*, we are uncertain where the narrative will eventually lead us. In *The Apprentice*, a greater part of the attraction for the audience is predicting who will get sacked in a formula that is exactly the same every week and series. The VO constantly reminds us what to expect, but we just don't know who will be fired or how. This is why the show works on a broadcast platform. It requires the audience to keep coming back weekly, which would not work for cinema.

In this section the narrative is effectively related to the platform used.

With *Anvil* and *HIM*, there are things like the conventional official band websites, with their band photos, blogs and downloads, and other sites that review the documentaries, but that add little to the documentary genre. The extensive *Apprentice* section on **www.bbc.co.uk**, however, has a lot more synergy with the actual programme because it expands the narrative, for instance it has interviews and more in-depth information about each contestant. It also offers Web 2.0 interactivity through message boards and a predictor device which allows viewers to predict who will be fired simultaneously with the live broadcast.

Here the discussion is extended to a new platform. Because this is not the primary platform for documentary, the discussion of the forms of websites is

questions & answers

briefer. However, it does seek to evaluate whether the new platform supports the documentary form effectively or not.

The Apprentice, like other high-profile competitive reality shows, provides a lot of content for tabloids, but this is treated as hard news using the 'inverted pyramid' structure. It is in the review and supplement sections, like the *Sunday Times Culture* magazine, or in subject-specialist magazines like *Kerrang!* that we would find a style of writing, such as the extended interview, and photojournalism that reflects and extends the original documentary form. *The Apprentice* is well served beyond the broadcast platforms; it is featured in *Radio Times* — a BBC publication. *Radio Times* usually runs a feature introducing the candidates before the series begins, which will include photos, interviews, quotes and commentary from celebrities to whet the appetite of the viewer and entice them into watching the show.

> This paragraph gives us the third media platform and continues in the same way as the previous website section, considering the form of print and how it relates to the example texts.

> Throughout the answer, the candidate shows thorough understanding and knowledge of the media forms and language used in documentary and hybrid forms. The answer details documentary approaches that are used by three different technologies (film, radio and TV) and explores the way in which documentary forms and texts are treated on two other platforms (web and print). The discussion of the different forms is fully supported throughout by reference to the case study texts (clearly indicated at the start) as well as other texts on different platforms. The writing is clear and well organised, using an appropriate style. The answer shows the candidate's confident understanding of how documentary and hybrid forms are used in different ways for different purposes. This is a clear A-grade response.

C-grade answer

I have studied documentary and hybrids by watching *Anvil*, a film about two heavy metal musicians, *HIM*, a radio documentary about a Finnish band and *The Apprentice*, a business-based 'reality TV' show.

> The opening clearly indicates the textual examples, although it could give a little more information, for example about the institutions.

Each of these films and programmes tells the audience that they use conventions of documentaries. They do this in slightly different ways. The two moving image examples use things like hand-held cameras. When a camera is hand held it does not look so professional as when it is on a tripod, so this makes people watching think that it must be more realistic, because there is not time to set up a fancy shot, you just have to film something as it happens and be prepared to follow the action. Sometimes you see this in fictional films, like horrors or thrillers, where a hand-held camera is used by a stalker to make it seem more real. The Radio 1 documentary on *His Infernal Majesty* can't use cameras so it uses lots of interviews with real people instead.

> 🖉 There is quite a good attempt to show the generic conventions of documentary that are used in the texts. This is heading in the right direction and indicates that the candidate has the right idea. However, the discussion does not widen out to include other key signifiers of the documentary genre, and there is a lack of detailed media language.

Each one of the documentaries uses soundtrack music. The two documentaries about bands obviously can use the music from the bands themselves, which makes things a bit more realistic, because it is what the bands would do anyway, even if they were not in a documentary. *The Apprentice* has loads of different musical styles which are used to tell us if things are going well for the contestants or not.

> 🖉 There is some building on from the previous section, but again the point being made lacks technical accuracy and is quite general.

Each of the examples has its own style of presentation. *Anvil* doesn't have anyone doing the voice-over, so there is more talking between the two main people, and sometimes it uses titles to tell us certain things like locations. *The Apprentice* and *HIM* both have presenters who explain what is happening next, which is useful for the audience.

> 🖉 This section is quite observant, and explains the points quite well. What is missing is a clear sense that the audience is being led to a particular reading of what is being shown.

All the texts tell different types of story. The most obvious one is *Anvil*, which follows the two musicians from being nearly famous, to being sad old losers, to starting to be famous again. The *HIM* documentary sort of tells the story of how the group got famous, with quite a few well-known people from other groups, like My Chemical Romance saying how *HIM* have influenced them. *The Apprentice* is not really a story at all, but it has got a narrative that follows the contestants each week to see who will eventually become Sir Alan's apprentice and get to work for him.

> 🖉 Here the candidate shows some understanding and uses the term 'narrative' in a relevant way, although this is somewhat undermined by continually referring to the 'story'.

The three texts have got websites that allow the audience to find out more about the film and programmes, or at least about the people shown in them. *Anvil* has a website that tells us what the group is doing, it has a YouTube clip of the film's trailer and it allows you to buy the film online. *HIM* has a similar website with all the usual conventions of a website. *The Apprentice* has a website that is part of the BBC's main website. It has different things from the other two, because it only exists as a TV programme, whereas the bands carry on after the documentaries. *The Apprentice* site has a lot of interactive things and info about the contestants that the audience will like.

The three texts also get represented in the press. For example, the tabloids always like to run stories about contestants in *The Apprentice*, especially digging dirt on them to make them look stupid. *The Apprentice* also gets a lot of coverage in *Radio Times*, which is owned by the BBC, so they can use it to promote the programme.

There are a number of Heavy Metal magazines, such as *Kerrang!* and *Metal Hammer*. These are the sorts of print platform that both *Anvil* and *HIM* would appear in, and fans of the groups would read these to find out more about the groups that they didn't get from the documentaries.

These last sections of the response cover other media platforms and make some good points. However, the difference in comparison with the A-grade piece is that the candidate has started to move away from the focus of the question — the forms, codes and conventions. The A-grade piece compares the effect other platforms have on the documentary form, whereas this response begins to concentrate more on issues such as audience appeal.

At its best, this answer applies knowledge and understanding of documentary codes and conventions in a satisfactory way, although in a number of places it provides more basic information that anyone with intelligence could give. It makes quite good reference across three different media platforms.

Some attempt is made to explain how the forms of documentary communicate, with some useful examples in places. The response has been written in a fairly structured way, it is quite easy to follow the points being made, and these points are mainly supported by useful examples from the case study. In some places, the written language becomes a little too informal. There is some use and explanation of media terminology, such as narrative, but in other places the language becomes somewhat basic. Overall, this is a C-grade response.

■ ■ ■

Question 2: media representation

How are people and/or places represented in the media products in your case study?

Candidates' answers to Question 2

The candidates' answers to this question use a music industry case study.

A-grade answer

My case study is based on the way that music genres and music events are handled on different media platforms. To answer this question, I will be referencing the Muslim hip hop magazine *The Platform*, the web presence of former *X Factor* winner Alexandra Burke and the BBC's multi-platform coverage of the Glastonbury festival.

Magazines have often been used for creating niche media products that appeal to specific audiences by being able to represent the target group effectively. *The Platform*, started as an underground magazine in 2006, is a good example of this.

section

Hip hop is a resilient and adaptable genre that has gone from its African-American New York roots to influence youth cultures from Bulgaria to Japan. *The Platform* takes the main elements of the hip hop demographic — mainly young people from ethnic and cultural minorities — and adds a specific religious dimension. The magazine states, 'our aim at *The Platform* is to promote Muslim and conscious music'. The magazine acknowledges certain earlier hip hop artists, such as Afrika Bambaataa, for their support of Muslim ideas. However, it is mainly concerned with representing hip hop as a form for expressing feelings about current issues for young British Muslims, such as dealing with post-9/11 hostility from the mainstream, as well as issues connected with being a genre that is often at odds with traditional Islamic values. One such issue that it addresses is the debate about the place of young female Muslims who are into hip hop, represented by acts such as Poetic Pilgrimage, but who are looked down on by some Muslims as going against the religion. These young women are shown wearing burkas but shot using strong stances and urban locations that are associated with more typical hip hop imagery.

> This section shows the candidate has a clear understanding of the relationship between the textual representations and the audience, which can be essential to the success of certain texts. Media vocabulary around the key concept of representation is very good, for example when exploring the demographic make-up, and through this aspect of representation the candidate considers cross-cultural issues effectively. This is something that the exam board is keen to encourage.

At the other end of the spectrum of representation of African-Caribbean and Asian women in popular music is the fifth *X Factor* winner, Alexandra Burke. She appears on several official websites — her own, the *X Factor* and MySpace, as well as many other unofficial sites.

The official site is dominated by images of her made-up, wearing revealing, expensive designer clothing and looking out at the viewer in a sultry manner. The point of the *X Factor* is to manufacture a star from an ordinary person. Therefore, these glamorous, sexy images are contrasted somewhat by the writing. The Twitter extracts are designed to show her as an accessible person dealing with the same issues that other young women face, whilst the news and Facebook entries emphasise an altruistic side through the charity concerts she is involved with.

Her MySpace homepage has similar imagery to the official site, and the biography describes her as 'the girl who never gives up', emphasising a success narrative. Further down the page, below her latest music video, is a clip titled 'Alexandra Burke says Hi' which shows her sitting on a sofa in a fairly ordinary-looking living room without her hair done and make-up on. This seems similar to the use of Twitter to make her seem like just an ordinary London girl.

> This aspect of the answer moves on to a different platform, and contrasts well with the first section. It shows a good detailed range of knowledge and understanding that is used to explore contrasts and possible contradictions within the representations.

The BBC's multi-platform representation of Glastonbury festival has coverage on TV, radio and the internet. As well as the focus on performers, there is also significant time and space given to the live audience and the location itself.

The audio and visual representations portray the majority of the audience at the event as being drawn from white young people, in their late teens and twenties, with a fairly even ratio of female and male. On the TV broadcasts particularly, the performances are interspersed with documentary style forays into the crowd to observe and interview the audience. These clips tend to focus on the most outlandish people, chosen for their bizarre dress and behaviour, which seem to be designed to reinforce the perception of the festival as edgy and alternative. However, it can be argued that the very presence of the BBC there as 'official broadcaster' means that the festival has become far more tame and conventional than it used to be.

The visual representation of the location tends towards clichés such as the sleepy rural life of people with strong West-Country accents drinking cider being contrasted with the sudden influx of wild, loud, urban youth. The TV presenters are seen wandering around in wellies and sitting on hay bales as if they are at a barn dance. Recently, this stereotyping has given way to a more subtle approach with a series of short documentaries interspersed with the music coverage, which offer a more balanced view of the people who work on the site all year round.

> This section is able to combine further consideration of the representation of people with the way the texts portray the location. It makes useful links between key concepts, by exploring how the representations impact, and are influenced by, the forms used, the institution and the audience. As well as observations of demographic representation, this section deals well with the ideas of stereotyping, which are central to representation issues.
>
> The answer covers a lot of ground in detail, showing that the candidate has a very good understanding of a wide range of representational issues, which is supported by good use of relevant vocabulary. It is well structured and leads fluently from one section to the other. The range of case study examples allows for a decent variety of representational issues to be covered across platforms.

C-grade answer

I have done a case study on music and the media. It covers Muslim hip hop, the *X Factor* and the Glastonbury festival.

To start with I want to look at the music magazine *The Platform*, which is for fans of hip hop who are also Muslims. This is print, so it is a different way of talking to the audience than TV or the internet. This magazine covers stuff about the hip hop scene but mixes it together with things like what happened on 9/11 and terrorism. Also it covers issues about being a young Muslim in a non-Muslim country, and how some of the things to do with hip hop go against being a Muslim. It has lots of articles about Muslim hip hop acts, even girl bands, which some older Muslims don't like.

🖉 This response covers some useful ground, but is far too general and unspecific. It describes what the text is about and some of the representations, but it does very little to explain the representations.

On the internet we can find Alexandra Burke, who was one of the winners of the *X Factor*, who is female and black. She has things on different sites. The official *X Factor* site shows her as being all made-up and glamorous, wearing expensive clothes and bling to make her look like a real pop star, like Cheryl Cole or Danni Minogue. There is also stuff about her on Facebook and Myspace, which also show her looking all made-up. This means that wherever you look on the internet to find Alexandra Burke, she will always look like a real pop star. This is because she was the winner of the *X Factor*, and that show is designed to turn ordinary people into pop stars, which is what she has become.

🖉 The points being made here tend to go in circles, rather than offer any useful analysis.

Glastonbury festival is the biggest music festival that happens in Glastonbury in Somerset. Every time it is on the BBC shows highlights from the shows on the telly. There is also stuff on Radio 1 and the internet, so Glastonbury festival gets a lot of coverage. It mainly shows top bands from the main stage, but also you get interviews with freaks and weird-looking people who are usually drugged up and covered with mud.

They show a lot of indie type bands or rock stuff. You probably wouldn't get Alexandra Burke playing Glasto, or have Muslim hip hop there. But having said that, they did get people like Lady GaGa playing on the main stage, and there was a bit of upset when Jay-Z was one of the main acts.

Mainly when you see highlights of Glastonbury on the TV you see loads of young people enjoying themselves in the big crowds. It is for young people to escape from the usual day-to-day of school or college, or for people in their twenties to have a few days off work to have a wild time and see some of their favourite bands, and the TV shows this really well with plenty of shots of the crowds dancing and singing, even in the mud.

🖉 This section has potential because some of the points it makes are valid. The problem is it that it leaves ideas hanging in the air without further explanation. It is as if the candidate expects the reader to know what they are talking about. It makes sense to compare the earlier examples (Muslim hip hop/*X Factor* winner) and explore why they would not be represented at Glastonbury. But the point about the controversy over Jay-Z, a top rapper/hip hop artist, performing at the festival is wasted.

Overall the response lacks depth. There is a sense that, because the candidate is dealing with an aspect of the media of which they have had previous knowledge and understanding, they have dealt with this superficially in media terms. For an examiner, the piece will come over as fairly basic with limited use of media terminology, which is frustrating as it hints at some really good points.

■ ■ ■

Question 3: media institutions

Consider the reasons why media products from your case study are present across a range of media platforms.

Candidates' answers to Question 3

The candidates' answers to this question use a lifestyle case study.

A-grade answer

My cross-media case study looks at lifestyle. I will be looking at the relationship between lifestyle magazines and broadcasting. I will also consider how the internet and computer gaming have expanded the possibilities of lifestyle marketing.

Magazines have produced lifestyle content for a long time, particularly titles aimed at women, such as *Woman* and *Woman's Own* (launched in the 1930s). These are published by IPC Media, which began in the 1960s. *Good Housekeeping* is a rival, which was first published in the UK in the 1920s. The UK publisher, National Magazine Company, produces mainly lifestyle brands aimed at women, such as *Cosmopolitan* and *She*, and claims a UK market reach of '61% of all ABC1 magazine-reading women aged 15–55'.

The 1990s saw a huge rise of around 60% in magazines being published. Lifestyle magazines were responsible for a large amount of this increase, including the rise of the 'lads' magazine, such as IPC's *Loaded*, followed in 2004 by *Nuts*.

> 🖉 This section covers institutions of the print platform effectively, supported by a number of relevant examples of texts and comparisons of publishers. It makes a link to the way in which institutions consider audience as market.

The success of these titles in the print format has not stopped media companies expanding to other platforms. The 90s' magazine boom was paralleled by increased cable and satellite broadcasting. New stations needed content, and the term 'masthead television' was used to describe the way that magazine titles began to expand into TV, with titles like *Good Housekeeping* providing programmes for Sky.

> 🖉 Here the answer compares and bridges between media platforms. This is extended in the next paragraph.

Lifestyle programming is popular with 'publisher broadcasters' who do not have their own production facilities, and have to commission independent production. These include satellite and cable companies as well as terrestrial broadcasters such as Channel 4, who commission lifestyle programmes because they are relatively cheap to produce.

Channel 4 broadcasts a large amount of lifestyle content that appeals to a wide audience, from retired people during the day to cookery, fashion and property make-over shows that go beyond the watershed.

section

Channel 4 revolutionised TV production by challenging the 'in-house' production methods of the BBC and ITV companies, and encouraging production by independents. The Broadcasting Act made it a legal requirement of the BBC to commission up to 25% of its content from independents. As a result, the BBC has followed Channel 4's lead into lifestyle programming produced by independents.

> ✍ The answer confidently explains the impact of wider media institutional issues on the subject, in this case independent commissioning.

Both broadcasters make the connection back to print through tie-in magazine publications, such as *Grand Designs* and *Gardeners' World*. Channel 4 uses independents for magazine production, whilst the BBC uses the magazine division of BBC Worldwide, the part of the corporation that is allowed to make a profit. Ironically, given Channel 4's influence on commissioning, it has had difficulties fulfilling its public service remit while being profitable, and there have been suggestions that it merges with BBC Worldwide, because of the latter's success as the commercial arm of a state-owned public service broadcaster.

> ✍ The discussion links back to the first platform considered in the answer, and adds a point about the relationship between different areas of the industry. This shows the depth and breadth of understanding required to reach the top end of the mark scale.

While lifestyle magazines and TV programmes have a web presence, these sites tend to be a convenient cross-media add-on, rather than an innovation. A more imaginative approach to lifestyle can be found in 'virtual world' role-playing games (RPGs) and 'online worlds' that bring Web 2.0 types of interactivity and community through web-based applications. For younger users, these games tend to be based in fantasy worlds, like Disney's Club Penguin, or Webkinz World. Many older users prefer to inhabit virtual worlds that more closely resemble their real experience, such as Second Life or There. For many players the possibility of trying out lifestyle products is part of the attraction. The marketing potential for this has been taken up by many businesses that operate in Second Life, such as Reebok, Kraft and Calvin Klein. However, brand copyright infringement is a problem that is hard to stop in these online games. The Sims is a virtual-world RPG that did have a web version, but closed it down. This could be seen as a safer option for businesses, as the game incorporates lifestyle features from companies like Ikea and H&M. On The Sims website there is a store where you can purchase home décor, DIY, clothing and hair products to use in the game. One of these is a game extra called Ikea Home Stuff which provides furniture items for Sims houses based on real Ikea products. There is a similar opportunity to go to a virtual H&M shop to buy fashionable clothing.

Manufacturers of lifestyle products and their advertisers are seeing new opportunities offered by gaming and its convergence with the internet for new ways of reaching audiences. Traditional magazine and broadcast adverts rely on aspirational representations, where the viewer has to imagine the lifestyle products shown in their own home. By providing content for user-generated productions that games like The Sims offer, advertisers are engaging with their audience in a much more creative and direct way.

> This last section goes beyond the confines of traditional media to explore innovations in the ways in which producers and advertisers use new media technology to reach their audience.

> The answer shows a full understanding and evaluation of reasons why the three different platforms are used to present lifestyle content, with an informed awareness of the commercial marketing opportunities that go along with this. There are detailed examples from more than three texts used to support the discussion, which engages in good explanations about the use of the different platforms. The expression of ideas is polished and effective, and the use of media ideas is assured.

C-grade answer

My case study is all about lifestyle, through things like women's and lads' mags, TV make-over shows and the internet-based game The Sims.

First of all magazines. There have been lifestyle-type magazines for ages. Things like *Woman* and *Woman's Own* have been around for more than 50 years. They are published by companies such as IPC and National. They have lots of lifestyle information in them, like make-up and cookery. In the 90s there came lads' mags, which had different lifestyle things in them like sex, football and gadgets.

> This answer shows some knowledge and understanding of what lifestyle content is, and shows some ability to use examples to illustrate this, although the examples and explanations do not have much detail.

You get a lot of lifestyle programmes on TV these days, Channel 4 and some of the BBC channels in particular. There are cookery programmes with people like Gordon Ramsay, Jamie Oliver and Heston Blumenthal, or fashion shows like *Trinny and Susannah* and Gok Wan's, and home make-over programmes like *60 Minute Makeover* and *Grand Designs*.

Channel 4 show a lot of these programmes because they were told by the government that they had to do this when they first started, to appeal to lots of different interests like retired people, and have a public service remit. The BBC saw what Channel 4 had done and that they were successful, so they copied the ideas when the government said that they had to change too.

> This section is overly reliant on 'filler' material — just listing the names of programmes is not enough. What is needed is an explanation of why this type of programming has become popular. On this point the candidate is quite vague. They know that legislation has had an impact on the genres of programme that have become popular, but they do not know enough detail to explain this point fully.

The BBC also produces magazines, so they make magazines that support the lifestyle TV programmes they make, like gardening and cooking magazines. Channel 4 also

has magazines to go with their programmes, like the *Grand Designs* magazine. This shows why the TV companies also make sure that they cover other platforms like print.

> ✏️ In a similar way to the previous paragraph, there is a hint at some useful information, but it is expressed basically, and the last point does not fully make sense without further explanation.

A completely new way of doing lifestyle media on the internet is The Sims. This is a computer game, where you can create your own character (avatar) and make them do stuff they would do in the real world. So you get your character to go to work and get some money and buy a house. This is where it is really clever, because this is real lifestyle where you have to decorate your house. So The Sims has an additional game add-on that you can buy — which makes money for them. This add-on is called Ikea stuff and it lets you buy pretend furniture for your Sims house. This means that you are not just watching what lifestyle you could have on the TV or in a magazine, but you're actually making the lifestyle yourself but in virtual reality. This means you could try out something from Ikea in your game and see if you like it before you buy it properly for your own house.

> ✏️ The point made here is good, although the written expression lets it down.
>
> Overall, compared to the A-grade piece, this is somewhere between satisfactory and basic in the way it shows knowledge and understanding, and what it reveals about the candidate's ability to analyse and explain the issues. Grammar and expression are also significantly weaker.

■ ■ ■

Question 4: media audience

Explore the ways that audiences consume and respond to media products across different media platforms.

Candidates' answers to Question 4

The candidates' answers to this question use a film fiction case study.

A-grade answer

To answer this question I will be referring to my case study on film fiction, which will mainly focus on the Bond film *Quantum of Solace*, on *Slumdog Millionaire* and on *Angus Thongs and Perfect Snogging*. I will explore the way that audiences relate to these films as cinema texts, and how they use websites and print texts to extend and enhance their enjoyment of the films.

When domestic video came out in the late 70s and cinema audiences declined, some people predicted the death of cinema. But with the development of multiplexes, cinema bounced back. Since then new media technology seems to have enhanced theatrical viewing rather than threatened it. The first decade of the twenty-first century saw a rise of more than 20% in the number of people going to the cinema in the UK.

> ✐ This opening indicates that the candidate has confident understanding of the historical context.

The Bond franchise has been around since 1962 and has had similar cycles in audience interest as the UK cinema industry. When *Quantum of Solace* was released in 2008 it achieved the highest opening weekend box office figures for any Bond film. This would suggest that audiences still want the experience of seeing a text that has been specifically made for the big screen in its original context.

A lot of the Bond films' appeal can be attributed to the cinematic experience, where the audience is immersed in the film world through the large screen, impressive surround sound, lack of other distractions and the dream-like quality of watching in a darkened space. Bond provides the audience with an exotic adventure fantasy, despite the replacement of the suave, sexist, alpha male with a relatively gritty, complex, self-reflecting Bond.

> ✐ A mixture of analysis of audience statistics and what the audience gets from the text shows detailed understanding of consumption patterns.

Slumdog Millionaire also offers the audience a sense of exotic cinematic spectacle; the narrative rushes the audience through a combination of *National Geographic*-style colour imagery and gritty urban ghettos, via fast-paced action and rich soundtrack. Part of the pleasure for the audience is being able to briefly, and safely, step into the representation of another culture that probably feels foreign but not wholly unfamiliar because of the 'Millionaire' game reference. This also raises questions of cultural imperialism — the way that Western film makers have made poor people from India appealing to a largely Western audience.

Angus Thongs and Perfect Snogging, on the other hand, appeals to its target demographic of younger teenage girls precisely because it reflects familiar territory. The appeal is less a spectacular cinematic event; it appeals more through allowing the viewer to enter right into the life and mind of Georgia, the central character.

> ✐ Plenty of detailed application of knowledge and understanding is shown through the three examples, with clear reference to cross-cultural issues raised by *Slumdog Millionaire*.

Print cannot compete with the sensory thrill of cinema, but it provides supporting content that the audience wants. Niche and cult audiences look to specialist magazines to provide detailed and specialist pre-release information, long before mainstream news media get their marketing packs.

Hardcore Bond fans look to film magazines, like *Empire*, to provide them with details of the latest production in anticipation of the release, and this makes them feel like they have elite access to privileged information.

Audiences looking for a more independent viewpoint might turn to *Little White Lies*, which claims to feature cutting-edge writing. The younger female teenage audience for *Angus Thongs and Perfect Snogging* is less likely to read a film magazine, preferring to read news, reviews and features about the film in a publication like *Sugar*, which would address them in a more appealing manner.

Because of Web 2.0 applications, the internet offers film audiences opportunities to interact and even create their own material. The Bond site, **www.007.com**, allows viewers to play games based on scenes from *Quantum of Solace*. Slumdog's site offers less, although it does, unsurprisingly, feature an interactive version of *Who wants to be a Millionaire?*

The *Angus Thongs and Perfect Snogging* site has lots of features to engage with, and effectively extends the appeal of the film by its visual style, links to sites like Bebo and MySpace, and has an imaginative message board where people can create some simple user-generated content like posting digital photos from mobile phones and leaving messages for friends. This site seems to offer its audience more gratification by treating them as digital natives because it expects them to demand more than the other sites do. This is supported by a visit to YouTube, where there are more examples of user-generated content, such as videos made by fans who re-enact scenes or show slide shows of visits to the set. As well as providing post-release material, more savvy film advertisers are employing user-generated material to create viral marketing campaigns, as in the case of *Batman: The Dark Knight*.

> The way the three platforms are utilised by the audience is effectively explored in a thorough and precise overview of the cross-media study. This is supported by a range of detailed examples. The answer is written clearly and effectively, and shows very good use of media terminology. Media ideas and debates, such as the increase of user-generated responses from some audiences, are confidently explained.

C-grade answer

My case study covers the way that audiences watch the films *Quantum of Solace* (James Bond), *Slumdog Millionaire*, and *Angus Thongs and Perfect Snogging*. It also looks at the way these films reach the audience through print and websites.

The experience of going to the cinema is on the rise in the UK, with more people visiting the cinema now than they did in the 1990s. Although people like to watch films on TV and DVD, this tells us that they also still enjoy the experience of going to the cinema too.

> The response starts well, giving a clear indication of the case study texts. The second paragraph attempts to give some historical context, but lacks useful details and supporting figures about audiences to support the point.

This is true of the James Bond series. *Quantum of Solace* was the most popular James Bond film at the cinema since they started in the 1960s. This tells us that people must like going to the cinema to experience what the Bond films have to offer, like big stars, big locations, action sequences, romance and good music.

The audience was probably attracted to similar sorts of things with *Slumdog Millionaire*, even though it did not have any big stars, except the lead character was recognisable from his role in the first *Skins* series. This film showed lots of very colourful images of India, which would be attractive to the audience, because it looks hot and interesting. It also has quite an adventurous story like the James Bond films, which would keep the audience gripped.

Angus Thongs and Perfect Snogging is aimed at a different audience of teenage girls. But they would like the film too because it is quite colourful and has stuff in it that teenage girls would probably like, like boyfriends and bands and going to parties. So girls would enjoy going to the cinema to see this film.

> The candidate tries to give reasons for the appeal of the films as cinema releases. The tendency is to concentrate on the appeal of the content of the films but does not extend to explore the experience that the cinematic platform offers to the audience.

Film audiences usually like to read things in magazines about films. This is because the magazines can tell you about films that will be coming out a long time before they actually arrive at the cinema. There are special film magazines like *Empire*, especially for film buffs. Depending on what is on the cover other people might read the magazines, like if Daniel Craig was shown for the latest James Bond film, then a Bond fan might buy the magazine to find out about the film. The same thing is true for *Angus Thongs and Perfect Snogging*, because some girls might have read the book. But in this case you are more likely to find stuff like this in girls' magazines rather than serious film magazines, which might not think it is worth doing an in-depth article for teenage girls. If you were a fan of *Who Wants to be a Millionaire*, or you liked Danny Boyle, the director, then you might read a magazine that had stuff about the film in it.

> This generally works as a response; it gives some relevant and useful information. Some of this is supported by examples, although other aspects are too general, and the overall expression of ideas is a bit limited.

On the internet there are quite a lot of things for fans of the films to do on the official websites, like on the *Quantum of Solace* site there are games where you are in an old aeroplane like in the film, being chased by the bad guys. On the *Slumdog Millionaire* site you can actually play *Who wants to be a Millionaire?*, but you can't win any money because the game is too easy, so it appeals to all ages. On the *Angus Thongs and Perfect Snogging* site there are lots of things that teenage girls will like, like being able to leave each other messages and blogs. These sites give the audience extra things to do once they have watched the films to keep them interested in the films themselves.

> The candidate has clearly learnt about the extras that are available on the internet, and explained these, and given a reason why they would appeal to the audience.

This is a satisfactory response, where the candidate shows some useful and relevant understanding of what appeals to audiences, tracing their interest across the different platforms. In some places the ideas are a bit simplistic and they are not fully supported by examples. They are also not developed into more sophisticated ideas to constitute the type of good detailed response that would be expected from someone who had studied media in some depth. Overall, this is a C-grade answer.

■ ■ ■

Practice and revision: how to prepare for the exam

Section A: unseen text

Preparing for this part of the test is relatively easy. You will need to find examples of texts that you have not seen or read before, such as a newspaper or web page, a recorded clip from a radio or TV show, or a section from a film, or a trailer. Use the four questions given in this guide, and see what you can write on each section in 15 minutes. You don't even need to do all four questions at once. Just keep practising what you can write in 15 minutes. When you have finished, compare your answers to the answers given earlier in this section. Although the form and text will be different, you can still see if you are using the same sorts of ideas in your own answers. You should aim to write 200–300 words in 15 minutes for each question in Section A. So remember to count up how many words you are writing each time.

Section B: case study

Using the ideas given in this guide for creating a case study, along with the work that you may be doing in school or college, put together your own study. Make sure that you have at least three examples for your initial platform, and that you consider how each of these examples can be extended onto two additional platforms. Don't forget, you can also give other examples in addition to your main texts to illustrate points that you want to make. Also remember that you are thinking about your case study through the key concepts, so make sure that you know about the media forms, the use of representation, the institutions and the audience for your study.

When you think you have gathered enough information, you can practise answering Section B questions — sample questions provided by AQA are listed below. You should aim to write 600–700 words in 45 minutes for Section B.

Section B: sample questions

Media forms

- Account for the similarities and differences in the codes and conventions used in the media products from your case study.

Representation

- How are people and/or places represented in the media products in your case study?

Institutions

- Consider the reasons why media products from your case study are present across a range of media platforms.
- What is the relationship between the media products in your case study and the advertising industry?
- Write a talk to present to media producers making a case for using a range of different media platforms to reach consumers.

Audience

- Explore the ways in which audiences consume and respond to media products across different media platforms.
- 'Audiences are no longer just consumers of media texts but producers.' To what extent is this true of the media products in your case study?
- To what extent do the media products in your case study do more than just entertain their audiences?
- Are the media 'dumbing down'? Discuss this question in relation to the media products in your case study.

appendix

Appendix 1

Unseen text example, music website

Appendix 2

Media audience research organisations

The following organisations provide audience research statistics for different UK media platforms, some of which are available to the general public:

TV broadcast
Broadcasters' Audience Research Board (**www.barb.co.uk**)

Print
Audit Bureau of Circulation (**www.abc.org.uk**)

National Readership Survey (**www.nrs.co.uk**)

Radio
Radio Joint Audience Research (**www.rajar.co.uk**)

Cinema
Film audience measurement and evaluation (**www.dcm.co.uk**)

UK Film Council (**www.ukfilmcouncil.org.uk**)

Internet
Nielsen NetRatings (**www.en-us.nielsen.com**)

Search Engine Watch (**www.searchenginewatch.com**)

Econsultancy (**www.econsultancy.com**)

Glossary

actuality: audio or visual recording of an actual event.

advertising revenue: the money media producers make from companies advertising through their products and services.

anchorage: the way that the meanings of images are fixed by use of a caption or voice-overs.

baby boomers: the largest population group, born between 1946 and 1964. They are important to media producers and advertisers because of their numbers and spending power.

brand: a company name or logo that represents values that the company and its products stand for. Branding aims to gain trust and recognition from customers.

brand loyalty: when customers trust and value a brand, they will keep going back to it rather than use other brands offering similar things.

cinéma vérité: an observational method of making a documentary. See also **modes of documentary**.

codes: parts of a media text that communicate. These can be:

    technical, e.g. a wide-angled shot to establish location

    symbolic, e.g. James Bond's car symbolises wealth and power

    linguistic (spoken or written), e.g. a newspaper headline

conventions: the usual or expected way of doing something, particularly the way codes are combined. See also **genre**.

convergence: combining separate things into one. A mobile phone converges a phone, camera, video and MP3 player.

demographics: a set of categories used to describe representation and audience, such as: age, gender, socio-economic status, level of education, political views, race, nationality, and religion.

diegesis: part of a story. For example:

    diegetic music is part of the story in a film, such music coming from a car radio that characters hear.

    non-diegetic sound, or soundtrack, is not part of the story and only the audience are aware of it.

dumbing down: where media content is made overly simplistic to appeal to the widest audience. See also **infotainment**.

format: a method of conveying information or content. This can be:

    technical, e.g. Blu-ray video recording formats.

    generic, e.g. the 'reality TV' format.

fragmentation: when something breaks into smaller parts, for instance the fragmentation of the terrestrial TV audience with the arrival of multi-channel viewing.

franchise: an idea, product or service that is sold on to other organisations, for example *X Factor* is franchised to US TV by Simon Cowell's Syco production company,

gatekeeping: where an elite group controls the selection, combination and distribution of media content. See also **mediation**.

genre: categories of media texts which are immediately recognisable to the audience. Genre acts as a template for the conventions that should go into a product.

high production values: a media product that has had a lot of money spent on all aspects of production.

horizontal/vertical integration: the ownership of a variety of aspects of an industry by media businesses and organisations.

    horizontal integration occurs when someone like Rupert Murdoch expands his ownership of businesses across platforms, such as newspapers, TV and the internet.

    vertical integration occurs when one company controls the whole chain of production, distribution and exhibition, and therefore monopolises the market.

infotainment: a media text that combines information and entertainment because producers think that audiences cannot handle pure information.

innovation adoption cycle: Everett Rogers' theory of how people take up new technology.

Kuleshov effect: the way two images are edited together to create a relationship or meaning in the mind of the viewer.

linear/non-linear:

    linear: a media text that has to be consumed from start to finish in the right order, e.g. a film.

    non-linear: a text that can be engaged with at any point for any amount of time, e.g. a website.

media platform: a specific technology that supports media content to address an audience, e.g. broadcast TV and radio, cinema, the internet, print.

mediation: the process of creating ideas and messages that are communicated, and represented, through language, technology and institutions to an audience.

modes of documentary: Bill Nichols' theory of documentary types such as expositional or interactive.

montage: a sequence of moving images, usually rapidly edited, to show an association of ideas.

narrative: the way in which content or a story is structured.

news values: the underlying reasons why certain stories are chosen to be in the news.

niche audience/niche marketing/segmentation: the way media producers and advertisers address very specific demographic groups.

on demand: providing media content when the audience wants it, rather than when media producers schedule it. See **scheduling**.

patterns of consumption: the ways that audiences are expected to use media.

preferred reading: how media producers want audiences to interpret a media text.

psychographics: marketing terms to describe consumer behaviour: succeeders, aspirers, reformers and mainstreamers.

public service broadcaster: a media broadcaster that by law has to provide a certain amount of programme content for all members of society.

publisher broadcaster: a broadcaster that commissions others to create content/ texts, rather than making it themselves.

scheduling: the times and days when media texts will be made available to the audience, as decided by the producers. See **on demand**.

synergy: when two or more media texts work together for the mutual benefit of both, such as a soundtrack by a well-known band that is used on a film.

target audience: the demographic description of who a text is designed to appeal to.

text: an individual media product such as a TV show, film, magazine or website.

user-generated content (UGC): media material created by members of the audience using a web-based application like YouTube.

uses and gratification: the enjoyment or satisfaction that audiences get from engaging with specific media texts.

Web 2.0: technologies and services available on the internet that allow audiences to participate actively and interact.